As our culture elevates self-actu
the default assumption is that su
costs. No surprise then that the
release from anxiety, and church becomes a seu ....-p
church life gets demanding, the exit beckons. How shockingly
counter-cultural is Christ's insistence that 'whoever wants to
save their life will lose it, but whoever loses their life for me will
find it.' This book is counter-cultural too. John Benton takes us
through Paul's letter to the Philippians, showing that discipleship
means commitment, and commitment involves sacrifice. Paul's
deep love for the church is evident throughout Philippians, and
John Benton's love for the local church shines through this short
book. Real joy comes when we are liberated from the endless
and futile quest for self-fulfillment, and give ourselves to Christ
and to His people.

Sharon James

Social Policy Analyst, The Christian Institute,
Author of several books, including *How Christianity Transformed the World*

John Benton reflects in a thoughtful and warm but also
challenging way on how churches and individual Christians have
become juvenile like the world rather than mature in Christ.
He draws six aspects of maturity from Philippians and lays out
practical ways in which we can pursue it. Underlying the whole
is a right concern that it is only mature churches that will be
able to stand in the coming storms. This foray into Philippians
would make an excellent basis for spiritual self-examination by
any individual or church and might work particularly well for an
eldership to read together as they reflect on their corporate life.

Garry Williams

Director, John Owen Centre, London Theological Seminary

Watch out cruise-control Christians—you will never look at Philippians the same way again! In *Church for Grown-Ups*, John Benton deftly draws out six expectations Paul had for the church at Philippi (quality, priority, community, integrity, stability, and generosity). Every member of the Body of Christ would do well to read and reflect upon these truths for maturity in Christ. I profited much from this study.

Flip Michaels
Associate Pastor, GraceLife Church, Hershey, Pennsylvania
Author of *Five Half-Truths: Addressing the Most Common Misconceptions of Christianity*

Church
For Grown-Ups

INTENTIONAL MATURITY
FOR GOSPEL CONGREGATIONS

John Benton

CHRISTIAN
FOCUS

paperback ISBN 978-1-5271-0680-2
epub ISBN 978-1-5271-0710-6
mobi ISBN 978-1-5271-0711-3

10 9 8 7 6 5 4 3 2 1

Published in 2021
by
Christian Focus Publications, Ltd.
Geanies House, Fearn,
Ross-shire, IV20 1TW, Scotland.
www.christianfocus.com

Cover design by Pete Barnsley

Printed and bound by
Bell & Bain, Glasgow

CONTENTS

To Central Fellowship Group 2020 – lockdown heroes

Introduction

There was a young lad named Greg who used to come to our children's club at church. When he was about seven years old someone asked him the classic question, 'Greg, what do you want to be when you grow up?' He answered straightaway, 'A film star.' Then he hesitated, reflected a moment, and added, 'But I'd get a stunt man to do the kissing.'

Now that Greg has grown up, his ideas have very much changed. He has become mature.

To stay immature is to miss out. To deliberately remain immature is not only inappropriate but foolish. Indeed, we realise, it might even be damaging. But today, I suggest, Christians of all ages have a problem with immaturity, both as individuals and as churches.

Such is the problem, that it is likely that even the word 'maturity' is a turn off for many people. The vocabulary of our times is loaded against it. 'Maturity' equates with being boring, never having fun, taking no risks, being middle of the road. But that is really a piece of propaganda which is perpetuated by our culture and stunts the spiritual growth of God's people.

Rightly understood, to be mature means to be at our peak in life. Wine that has matured over the years is at its best and tastes wonderful. Estate agents will speak about a house having a 'mature garden' by which they mean it is well populated with healthy plants and trees which are going to produce flowers and fruit of the best quality for coming years. A settled immaturity is likely to mean a diminished life and a lack of fruit.

INDIVIDUALS

As *individuals* we live in a secular society which believes that this life is all there is. Here and now is our one chance of enjoying ourselves. The Covid-19 pandemic was a shock to the system for our world because it pushed death high up the agenda. Avoiding thoughts of mortality our culture therefore idolises youth and generally does not want to grow up. It wants to stay young. In a way, that's fine. However, immaturity generally goes with youth. So immature behaviour – moodiness, making and breaking friendships every week, ducking responsibility, last minute changes of plans on a whim at the flick of a text, expecting to be entertained, a sense of entitlement – somehow is looked upon as normal by our society.

So sometimes we see adult young people behaving like children. It can be looked upon as cool for 'twenty and thirty somethings' to act like kids – for men to shirk what needs to be done because they are hooked on computer games or for grown women to be as addicted to Facebook and Instagram as any sixth-former. And Christians can get caught up in the flow of all this to the detriment of growing up into Christlikeness.

CHURCHES

As *churches* too we face an increasing problem of immaturity. Church culture has for many years been in the process of being reshaped by youth culture. Old is bad, young is good. It's the culture of emotionalism, the culture of entertainment, the culture of leisure options, the culture of excitement. Even secular sociologists have begun to speak about 'the juvenilisation of Christianity'[1] and to study how church is now music-driven, just as youth culture in the world is music-driven, rather than conscience-driven.

Church has become concerned with style over substance. It isn't just young people who are attracted to church by the 'performances' of the wonderful worship band, or the big-name preacher with his superbly crafted and entertaining sermon. There seems little by way of self-denial and taking up the cross. Knuckling down to take responsibility to serve a church come-what-may, appears to be an attitude which is almost frowned upon.

To remain immature, or even to promote immaturity, may bring short-term gains but in the long term it will do immense damage to the church. So, whether we are chronologically older or younger, we need to think about 'what is a mature church?', and how to journey to maturity as churches. And when God works to bring His people to maturity, He does not make them boring, but He does give them wisdom, creativity and godliness which honours Christ above all things.

PHILIPPIANS

Paul's epistle to the Philippians will help us as we think about maturity. The church in Philippi was going on well with Christ

---

1   See for example, *The Juvenilization of American Christianity*, by Thomas E. Bergler (Eerdmans, 2012). Bergler defines juvenilisation as 'a way of experiencing Christianity which conforms to the patterns of adolescence in our culture.'

(1:3), but it also had capacity for improvement (1:9-11; 4:2-3).[2] Reading his letter we find that Paul rejoices in the progress that the church in Philippi has made, but he still looks for further growth and blessing (4:17).

So his letter provides a suitable guide for us as we look for people and churches to 'grow up' in Christ. There are three things to say as we begin this brief engagement with the epistle.

First, though spiritual maturity is often rightly summed up under the great Christian triad of faith, hope and love (1 Cor. 13:13), at a practical level this topic can be opened up in a variety of ways. All we are doing is seeking to pick up on six broad themes which encourage the fullest development in Christ. They are the themes of quality, priority, community, integrity, stability and generosity that flow from the good news of Jesus Christ. These themes emerge quite naturally from the book of Philippians and will give us an idea of what a fully-fledged, seasoned, 'grown-up' Christian congregation should look like.

Second, individual maturity and congregational maturity go together. Being in a 'grown-up' fellowship helps us to grow up spiritually as individuals. And the reverse is true. A mature church is dependent on the presence of a number of mature Christians being committed to it; you can't have a spiritually grown-up church without spiritually mature members.

Third, a key reference to maturity in Philippians is 3:12-15: 'Not that I have already obtained all this, or have already been made perfect, but I press on to take hold of that for which Christ Jesus took hold of me....' Even Paul, the great apostle, sees himself as still on a journey, not having arrived. But he goes on to encourage us all to follow his lead concerning maturity. 'Whatever you have learned or received or heard from me, or

---

2   Unless otherwise indicated, Scripture references are to the Book of Philippians.

seen in me – put it into practice' (4:9). We are still works-in-progress. To quote Ralph Martin, 'It is a maturity which seeks ever greater maturity.'[3] The apostle is pleased with where they have reached, but he is looking for them to kick on in their Christian lives. So, whether it is by way of maturity as individuals or as churches, please don't hear me as telling you whether or not you have 'arrived'. None of us have. I'm simply trying to point us in the right direction for the journey.

With these things in mind, let's look afresh at Philippians.

---

3   *Philippians*, Tyndale New Testament Commentaries, by Ralph Martin, (IVP, 1987) p. 158.

Chapter 1

The Mature Church's Quality

The film *La La Land* won rave reviews in 2016. It was, in many ways, the screen event of the year with its fabulous music, dancing and its unusual boy-meets-girl storyline. It stars Ryan Gosling as Sebastian, a gifted jazz pianist, and Emma Stone as Mia, trying to make it as an actress. They meet in Los Angeles, in a traffic jam, but somehow they are attracted to each other as they pursue their dreams and separately try to climb the uncertain ladder to success.

But having encouraged her, through down times, not to give up on a career in theatre, Sebastian manages to miss her play. She cannot forgive him and ends their relationship, gives up on her dream and moves back home. However, he gets a call from a casting director who had seen Mia's play and wants to contact her to audition for a role in a film. Sebastian drives for miles, finds where she is living, and persuades Mia to take the audition. She lands the part. But though they profess they will always love each other, the relationship finishes.

Five years later, she is a prominent actress but is married to another man and has a daughter. When they are out for the evening, she and her partner stumble across a jazz bar and go in.

It turns out to belong to Sebastian. He notices Mia and begins to play 'their song' on the piano. A dream sequence follows which is meant to encapsulate 'what might have been' between them. But the reality is that they both put success and their careers first, and their romance had to take a back seat. Mia leaves the bar with her husband and that is where the film ends.

The film won in six categories at the Oscars.

What was striking about this musical was that in many ways it broke the mould. It had tender scenes and great music, but it was totally different from the classic musical romance. Traditionally, the couple fall in love, face many troubles and temptations, but win through and set aside everything else so that they can be together, 'happily ever after'. He gets his girl. She gets her man. The message is that romantic love is what life is about.

CHANGED TIMES

But in the changed times of the twenty-first century, *La La Land* was saying something different. It was in effect saying the opposite. Its message was that pursuing your personal dream – for fame, for career, for whatever you see as success – trumps romance. 'Life is first and foremost about you, not other people, even those for whom you have a deep affection.' That was the point. Romantic love must take second place. This scintillating piece of cinema is unashamedly me-centred in its philosophy.

We live in the society of the self. We are encouraged to think of ourselves primarily as individuals. The world has always been self-centred to some extent, but it was often hidden under a veneer of 'niceness'. Today's more honest generation is prepared to be explicit. Life is about you and your bucket-list.

But the call to Christians, and God's calling for the church, is to be different from our culture. There is a quality which should make us stand out. It is a quality of striking beauty which challenges the self-centred view of the world and embarrasses it. And we find that quality woven deeply into the opening of Philippians. Here are the first eleven verses:

> *Paul and Timothy, servants of Christ Jesus, to all God's holy people in Christ Jesus at Philippi, together with the overseers and deacons:*
>
> *Grace and peace to you from God our Father and the Lord Jesus Christ.*
>
> *I thank my God every time I remember you. In all my prayers for all of you, I always pray with joy because of your partnership in the gospel from the first day until now, being confident of this, that he who began a good work in you will carry it on to completion until the day of Christ Jesus.*
>
> *It is right for me to feel this way about all of you, since I have you in my heart and, whether I am in chains or defending and confirming the gospel, all of you share in God's grace with me. God can testify how I long for all of you with the affection of Christ Jesus.*
>
> *And this is my prayer: that your love may abound more and more in knowledge and depth of insight, so that you may be able to discern what is best and may be pure and blameless for the day of Christ, filled with the fruit of righteousness that comes through Jesus Christ—to the glory and praise of God.*

CHRISTIAN LOVE

The overarching quality that should pervade every Christian and every church is Christ-like love. It's not the same as romantic love, though, arguably, it overlaps with it. It is not about thinking of yourself first. It is about deep affection which sacrifices itself for the good of others. This love really is the most important thing in the world.

In effect, the Bible turns the tables on *La La Land* and says that I might be the most gifted person, the most famous person in the world, but without love I am a nothing in God's sight. A church's growth may be breath-taking. It may become the biggest and most successful congregation in the world, but without love it is just a big fat spiritual zero (see 1 Corinthians 13).

Christian maturity recognises this and goes all out to pursue Christian love in the name of Jesus. Let's see how this underlies all that Paul says as he begins his letter to the church at Philippi.

PEOPLE IT'S EASY TO PRAY FOR

There are some people who are easy to pray for! When you get down on your knees you think of them and a spontaneous smile comes to your face. As you remember each person, maybe in a group, you say in your heart, 'What lovely folk!'

That was Paul's experience as he prayed for the members of the church in Philippi, a leading city of ancient Macedonia. The reason he found it so easy to pray for them was because he loved them and they loved him. (Sadly, it's not so easy to pray for some people!) In fact, Paul loved them so much he didn't like being away from them. He 'longed for them' (v. 8), but it was a joy to pray for them (v. 4).

These opening verses of the letter relate something of Paul's prayer-life for this church and it is shot through with Christian love. The love in the church made it a quality church in Paul's eyes and he couldn't help but love them in return.

HELPING LOVE

The love of the Philippians was practical. 'In all my prayers for all of you, I always pray with joy because of your partnership in the gospel from the first day until now' (vv. 4, 5). The word 'partnership' can apply to being in a business venture together and sharing your resources. It can be translated 'fellowship' – being 'in the same boat' and practically sharing your life with others. And that's how it was from the very beginning of the church in Philippi. They wanted to help Paul. The first Christian convert in Philippi was the businesswoman Lydia. As soon as she was baptised she invited Paul and his companions to her home. '"If you consider me a believer in the Lord," she said, "come and stay at my house." And she persuaded us' (Acts 16:15). She helped through hospitality. The Philippian jailer who was converted through the earthquake that hit the prison in the town, was of the same outlook (Acts 16:34). And from there the church had backed Paul and his mission to the hilt. They helped him, often sending money and supplies to him on his missionary journeys (Phil. 4:15, 16). Their love wasn't just words, it was practical.

HEARTFELT LOVE

The care of the Philippians for Paul and his prayerful care for them could not be further from 'cold charity'. There was warm affection between them. Their love for him had deeply penetrated Paul's emotions. 'I have you in my heart; for whether I am in chains or defending and confirming the gospel, all of you share in God's grace with me. God can testify how much I long for all of you' (vv. 7, 8). This is heartfelt love. What particularly touched Paul was the fact that even when he was in prison and *persona non grata* with many others, they stuck with him and kept providing for him and so sharing in his work. They obviously had a deep affection for him, and he for them.

HALLMARK LOVE

The love of the Philippians had been produced by the gospel and was the hallmark that they were genuine Christians. In Paul's prayer that their love would continue to increase, shaped by wisdom and godliness, love is described as 'the fruit of righteousness that comes through Jesus Christ' (vv. 9-11). Having experienced for themselves the love of God, in having all their sins forgiven and righteousness (right standing) before God given them through Christ, they could not help but love others just as God had loved them. This is the sign that their faith is real. It had been given to them from heaven – the world of love. Their practical love is the reason why Paul is confident 'that he who began a good work in you will carry it on until the day of Christ Jesus' (v. 6).

This Christian love is the quality that ought to characterise every Christian and every church. It is 'the most excellent way' (1 Cor. 12:31), without which there is no maturity in Christ. Paul sees love as the top-most height of true Christianity. 'And now these three remain: faith, hope and love. But the greatest of these is love' (1 Cor. 13:13). Because God is love, a loving church is where God feels at home (1 John 4:12). That makes for a grown-up church.

LOVE MAKES THE DIFFERENCE

This is the quality which makes the church different.

A few years ago our church began to run a 'holiday at home' for older people each summer. It lasts for three days. We reorganise the church into a hotel lounge and restaurant. In the 'lounge' there are newspapers, board games, crafts and general space to sit and chat. There are musical items and illustrated travel lectures and a short gospel talk each day. In the 'restaurant', morning coffee is served; a great lunch and an afternoon cream tea come later. Young people from the church get involved as waiters and waitresses. On the last day, weather permitting, we take the older folk out to a lovely Surrey village green for a picnic and tea in the cricket pavilion.

Not many years ago, an older couple, who had never been to the church before, came for the first time. They were interesting, chatty people who had seen a lot of the world. They had once run a business in the town and then spent some years travelling Europe in a camper van. They got to know a few of our people and enjoyed themselves, but they were not quite sure what to make of the church and what they heard.

We had come to the very end of the 'holiday'. We had sung a few songs and enjoyed tea and cake in the pavilion. Our M.C. had said 'thank you' to everyone for coming and that he hoped they had all experienced a happy few days together. He had just said 'Goodbye', and people had begun to stir themselves to go, when the husband of this couple got to his feet and banged a spoon on the table, drawing everyone's attention. We wondered what he was going to say.

He began to speak. 'We have never seen anything like this,' he said, 'it has been so lovely for us.' Tears began to roll down his cheeks. 'It's as if my wife and I have met a new race of people.' He went on, 'I've never seen young people looking after older ones like this. I didn't think young people like this existed anymore.' And then he said, 'My wife and I just want to say thank you. I don't know why you do this, but from what I've heard this week, perhaps I'm beginning to understand.' We were all very moved and he sat down.

They started coming to church on Sunday mornings, and about six months later the Lord saved first the wife under the preaching of the word and later the husband. But it was the love of the church that drew them in the first place. The world can be a cold and lonely place. Especially this is the case when it is dominated by a 'me first' spirit. But Christian love is like a fire and it draws people in towards the warmth of God's salvation in Christ.

The quality that should characterise the church is love.

THREATS TO LOVE

That's how the Philippian church was. That's how every church should be. But frequently that is sadly not how things are in reality. So we must ask a question. What kinds of things cause us to drift from this ideal or even lose sight of it?

First, we have a problem with *ourselves*. It goes without saying, that we have a sinful nature. Even though we are Christians and we fight it, sin still dwells in us. 'If we say we have no sin we deceive ourselves and the truth is not in us' (1 John 1:8). And sin is chronically self-centred. It is about love of self and so works against love for others. We are the kind of people who expect lots from others but are very good at cutting ourselves lots of slack. We need to be aware of this tendency in ourselves. We are naturally wayward people.

Second, there can be a problem caused by *churches*. For some churches, their top priority is to be doctrinally sound. In itself there's nothing wrong with that. We do need to stand for the truth of the gospel and not compromise on what the Bible teaches. But sometimes this concern for truth has been at the expense of love. It doesn't need to be like this, but often it is. The Puritan Samuel Ward has some very challenging words as he comments on Jesus lovingly washing His disciples' feet: 'The more men know and the less they do, the more they dishonour God.'[1] We can know our doctrine thoroughly but without love we are nothing (1 Cor. 13:2).

Third, there is a problem in our *culture*. There are a lot of things in the contemporary world, more than I can list, which reinforce the self-centred attitude. They encourage us not just to take 'selfies', but to be 'selfies'. We have already mentioned

---

1   *Voices from the Past: Puritan Devotional Readings*, Volume 1, Edited by Richard Rushing, (Banner of Truth, 2009), p. 107.

this in connection with films like *La La Land*, but we can point out quite a few more sources of self-centredness. Here are some examples:

- Much of today's digital *technology* is specifically aimed at the individual and promotes an individualistic attitude in us. Laptops and iPhones are personal things. They are for our convenience. They enable us to work on our own and play on our own. With a few passwords, no-one else is allowed in. We inhabit our own personal virtual world.

- Concern for *fitness and fashion* is very much about us. We want to look at ourselves in the mirror and be able to admire ourselves. We want to look good and so feel good – about ourselves. It is about caring for and pleasing ourselves. Even if we do not consciously think of it, this reinforces a certain focus on ourselves rather than other people.

- At work we are told we must *be professional*. In a sense that is right. We should be on top of our jobs. But that concept of being professional, especially in our engagement with others, frequently amounts to staying at a distance from people and not allowing ourselves to be too sympathetic or get emotionally involved. 'Stick to the protocol, be clinical and ignore your feelings.' It actually encourages us to be less than human and to treat other people as if they weren't human. God made us with emotions and to feel for others. But 'being professional' doesn't allow that.

Such 'selfie' ideas can spill over into our lives as Christians and subtly move us away from showing love towards others, even within the church. But to show love is to be like Jesus. To be full of love is therefore to be mature as a Christian. To lack love or to suppress love is not to have grown-up spiritually.

PAUL'S PRAYER

Paul has been telling us how much he enjoys praying for the church in Philippi. But what does he pray for them? What is the main content of his prayers? It should not surprise us. He says, 'And this is my prayer: that your love may abound...' (v. 9).

This prayer doesn't come out of nowhere. Paul has already been reflecting on their love to him and his love for them. For this loving church he is praying that their love might increase. They are already excelling in love, but Paul knows that the way forward is yet more love. He wants love not just to grow to a certain limit, but to grow – in fact to abound – more and more. There is to be no plateauing off. It is to grow and keep on growing. This is another indication of just how important love is for the Christian and for a church. The apostle looks for a love which keeps overflowing and cascading into the lives of others.

But such love does require to be channelled rightly. The way Paul's prayer unfolds shows that he is looking for their love to have three particular characteristics to make sure it always flows in the right direction.

Love – shaped by wisdom: He is praying that 'your love may abound more and more in knowledge and depth of insight' (v. 9). Love between Christians is to be shaped by a love and knowledge of God, not only in the head but in the heart. Our love should parallel what we know of God's love. That will give an ability to perceive what God wants. Love wants to bless others, but it can't always please others. It will be what God sees as best which alone will bring blessing to our friends in the long run.

Love – shown by purity: There should be a kindly passion about Christian love. But wise love is able 'to discern what is best and be pure and blameless' (v. 10). We want to pat people on the back in their triumphs, hold their hands through trouble, hug them in their tears. But such tactile expressions of affections can go too far. Christian love is passionate but always pure. The early Christians kissed each other, but with holy kisses (2 Cor. 13.12)!

Love – sustained by hope: Love is hard work sometimes. People do not always appreciate it when we try to help. Sometimes we get it wrong. Then we feel discouraged. But there is a time coming when love won't be so difficult. There is an end in view. We keep going 'until the day of Christ Jesus' (v. 10) – the day when Jesus returns, and the world and we are transformed. We can look forward to then and it will give us strength to keep going. On that day the Lord will judge how we have lived our lives, and such love as Paul has in mind will bring the Lord's approval.

It is such love which glorifies God and displays just how much the gospel can really change us for the better. It shows the goodness of God. Paul wants us to be filled with such love, which is 'the fruit of righteousness that comes through Jesus Christ – to the glory and praise of God' (v. 11).

Pray for love

At this point I could start trying to give all kinds of practical tips about love. But I won't, and there is a reason for not doing so.

The note which is obvious, but which we can easily miss from these verses is this. Such love grows through praying for each other. It is the fruit of the gospel, the fruit of God's work in us. We can try too hard. We can try to be loving in our own strength – in the flesh rather than in the Spirit. That is one of the ways love goes wrong. We become proud of how loving we are. Our self-centred hearts can even use love to inflate our own ego. We want to be seen as superstars of love. So we become religious prigs rather than humble servants. That's the way of the flesh and that is the way we will go unless God helps us. So we must pray.

There is an old saying from Islam I have come across which sadly can be true: 'The holier the city the wickeder the people.' That is where self-help religion leads. It can be true of some churches. We want our churches to stay a million miles from that.

True Christian love must be the distinguishing quality of a mature church. It is so different from the society where self is the centre. But only God can work such love in us. So we must pray.

If you are a church member, pray for your church to become a loving church. And if it is already a loving church pray that its love may 'abound more and more'.

If you are a pastor, you may be thinking about how to build your church. Before you think about quantity, think about quality. Before thinking about a sizeable congregation, think about a loving congregation, and pray that it will happen.

Chapter 2

The Mature Church's **Priority**

I remember, as a young married man, the day we brought home our first baby from the maternity unit in the hospital. It was the day I grew up. The sense of responsibility fell upon me. Here was a little bundle of life who depended on me (and my wife, of course) providing for him. I had to take life seriously now. Other things, even good things, had to move down my agenda. My priorities had to be reordered. I needed to stop being a perpetual student and get a job. I had to become a breadwinner.

Here we look at priorities. A mature person knows they can't do everything. Choices have to be made. Wise people know that they may even have to set aside things they would like to do in order to focus on things they need to do. They do this to serve a greater purpose.

As Christians we have been called to put the things of Christ first in our lives. He is to be our priority. He died so that we might live. And therefore it is only right that we now live for Him and His concerns. So with this in mind, let's jump into the subject of priorities as found in Philippians 1:12-26:

Now I want you to know, brothers and sisters, that what has happened to me has actually served to advance the gospel. As a result, it has become clear throughout the whole palace guard and to everyone else that I am in chains for Christ. And because of my chains, most of the brothers and sisters have become confident in the Lord and dare all the more to proclaim the gospel without fear.

It is true that some preach Christ out of envy and rivalry, but others out of goodwill. The latter do so out of love, knowing that I am put here for the defence of the gospel. The former preach Christ out of selfish ambition, not sincerely, supposing that they can stir up trouble for me while I am in chains. But what does it matter? The important thing is that in every way, whether from false motives or true, Christ is preached. And because of this I rejoice.

Yes, and I will continue to rejoice, for I know that through your prayers and God's provision of the Spirit of Jesus Christ what has happened to me will turn out for my deliverance. I eagerly expect and hope that I will in no way be ashamed, but will have sufficient courage so that now as always Christ will be exalted in my body, whether by life or by death. For to me, to live is Christ and to die is gain. If I am to go on living in the body, this will mean fruitful labour for me. Yet what shall I choose? I do not know! I am torn between the two: I desire to depart and be with Christ, which is better by far; but it is more necessary for you that I remain in the body. Convinced of this, I know that I will remain, and I will continue with all of you for your progress and joy in the faith, so that through my being with you again your boasting in Christ Jesus will abound on account of me.

In this section we meet the over-riding commitment to Christ and His gospel and the priority of spreading the gospel which the apostle Paul himself has. This is strikingly prominent.

Paul is in prison in Rome, but in verses 12-14, though his circumstances are bad, all he cares about is the fact that the gospel has been advanced: 'Now I want you to know, brothers and sisters, that what has happened to me has really served to advance the gospel' (v. 12). He probably had in mind that he could witness to his Roman guards from his prison cell. The point is that the gospel takes priority over his circumstances.

In verses 15-18 we find that Paul is not universally liked – even by Christians. Some were trying to cause trouble for him. But, nevertheless, he is saying: 'But what does it matter? The important thing is that in every way, whether from false motives or true, Christ is preached. And because of this I rejoice' (v. 18). The gospel comes first, above his reputation.

Then in that classic passage in verses 19-26, we find that though Paul's future seems uncertain – he might live, he might die – nevertheless his great concern is that the cause of Christ might progress: 'I eagerly expect and hope that I will be in no way ashamed, but will have sufficient courage so that now as always Christ will be exalted in my body, whether by life or death. For to me, to live is Christ and to die is gain' (vv. 20-21). So the gospel of the Lord Jesus even takes priority over his own life.

It's bigger than his circumstances. It is bigger than his reputation. It is bigger even than his life. The gospel is the great priority for Paul. But the point to notice is that the Philippian church has begun to share that same commitment, that same priority. Spreading the gospel, which brought the love of God into their lives, now has become top of their agenda.

We see this as Paul rejoices in their partnership in the gospel (1:5). He rejoices that whether he's in prison or out of it they are right behind him in his work (1:7). Later in the epistle, he tells us there was no other church which supported the missionary apostle financially in the way the Philippians did (4:15). Through their wallets and debit cards they were putting the gospel in first place as a church. Even though Paul is in prison, they are still helping him and his mission. They were beginning to be like Paul

– mature. Their top priority was in any way they could to serve Christ through helping to spread the gospel.

WHAT ARE YOUR PRIORITIES IN LIFE?

A philosophy professor at a seminary stood in front of his class with a large, empty mayonnaise jar. He proceeded to fill it with rocks which just squeezed through the neck. Then he asked the class if it was full. They said it was. But it wasn't. Next, from under his desk, he picked up a box of gravel and poured it into the jar. The gravel, of course, found its way into the spaces between the rocks. 'Is the jar full now?' he asked. The students agreed it was. But it wasn't.

He picked up a box of sand and poured the sand a little at a time into the jar, shaking it vigorously in between each new dose. The sand filled whatever empty space there was left. 'Is it full now?' A unanimous 'Yes!'

The professor then produced a cup of tea from under the table and proceeded to empty the entire contents into the jar. The class laughed.

'Now,' said the professor, 'think of this jar as your life. The rocks are the really important things – the big things that really matter, the things you feel are worth living and dying for. The gravel is the things that don't matter quite so much – like your job, or your house or your car. The sand is everything else – the small stuff, where you go on holiday, what toothpaste you use etc. If you pour gravel and sand into the jar first,' he continued, 'they will fill the jar so there is no room for the rocks. The same goes for your life. If you spend all your time and energy on insignificant stuff, you will never have room for the things that are really important. So set your priorities. Put them first. The rest is just sand.'

At that point one of the students raised her hand and asked what the cup of tea represented. 'I'm glad you asked that,' said the professor smiling. 'It just goes to show that no matter how full your life may seem, there's always room for a nice cup of tea!'

If you don't first put in place in your life the things that really matter, you will find there's no room for them. Your days will be filled – but with things which are of secondary importance. You will get to the end of your life and wonder what you achieved. The lesson of the mayonnaise jar is a good lesson. Is serving Christ, and doing whatever you can in your situation to help spread the gospel, your top priority as an individual? Is it the top priority of your church? Because if it's not, you will be immature, your life and your church will be busy with sand and gravel. You will not have grown up.

WHY HAS CHRIST LEFT THE CHURCH ON EARTH?

Why doesn't the Lord just take us all to heaven the moment we get saved? After all, we worship God on earth, but we will do it better in heaven; we progress in sanctification here, but we will be perfectly holy in heaven; we enjoy loving fellowship here, but our love will be far greater in heaven. So why does He leave us on earth?

The answer is this – because there is one great thing we can do on earth which we can never do in heaven, and that is to reach the lost, to share the gospel and build up gospel churches. That is what we are here for. This idea, or something like it, shapes Paul's thinking here in Philippians. He is more than happy to die and be with Christ, but he realises there is important work to do on earth for the gospel and for the church. 'I desire to depart and be with Christ, which is better by far; but it is more necessary for you that I remain in the body…and will continue with all of you for your progress and joy in the faith' (vv. 24-25). And a mature church takes that seriously: 'Go and make disciples of all nations, baptising them in the name of the Father and of the Son and of the Holy Spirit,' commands the Lord Jesus (Matt. 28:19).

WHAT ARE THE OBSTACLES TO THIS GOSPEL PRIORITY?

There are many things to hinder us – including our remaining sin and wayward hearts. But a big challenge to this priority comes from the consumer society in which we live. Our cultural environment influences us. The message of consumerism attacks our commitment at three main points.

First, consumer society encourages you, as we have seen already, to make yourself, your well-being, your first priority. 'Top of your list should be your career, your family and your pleasures,' says the world. But Jesus warned us that even our families must not take priority in our lives over commitment to Him: 'If anyone comes to me and does not hate his father and mother, his wife and children, his brothers and sisters – yes, even his own life – he cannot be my disciple' (Luke 14:26).

Second, consumer society, which is fundamentally secular, offers you all kinds of material things to choose from to fill your life with, instead of meaningful priorities. Consumerism literally spoils us for choice. There are any number of foods we can eat, fashions we can wear, foreign holidays we can buy. The contemporary world even offers us different 'lifestyles' which it encourages us to opt for. But, amid all this choice Jesus has called us to seek first God's kingdom and His righteousness (Matt. 6:33). He and His kingdom must come first.

Third, consumer society tells you that personal choice and freedom to choose is what life is all about. Life is for you doing what *you* want. The corollary of this which follows is, 'Don't get too committed to anything. Commitment narrows your options. So hang loose. Don't get too involved. Keep different doors open.' It encourages us to hang loose. But by contrast, the Bible tells us that real life comes through knowing God (John 17:3), who calls us to love Him above everything else, with everything we are and have (Mark 12:29-30). So Jesus warns us against continually sitting on the fence. We must choose and enter through the narrow gate and pursue the path (Matt. 7:13).

The consumer society pushes us to focus on ourselves – not Christ, not His gospel, not His people. Influenced by this, the result is that church and the gospel are often treated, even by its members, as a hobby, rather than their life's calling. The sand and the gravel take over. But Christian maturity is Christ-focused, church-focused and gospel-focused.

WHAT HAPPENS WHEN WE LOSE FOCUS?

Here are a few obvious examples.

Sunday worship is downgraded. These Christians I have in mind – at least I hope they are Christians – are often very flexible when it comes to their time. There's so much to choose from. They want to fit everything in. This translates into them being quite irregular about church on a Sunday. In one large church I know, the elders reckon that on any one Sunday a third of their congregation is elsewhere. The priority of sport and children's parties or going away for the weekend with the caravan, have taken over to such an extent in some churches that the idea of just one service on a Sunday is now very common. Twice is too much. Who wants to worship God and hear His Word twice? Who wants to keep a whole day for the Lord? After all, He's only God (!).

Evangelism gets sidelined. The consumer society can lead even zealous Christians to lose their evangelistic edge. It frames everything in terms of this life. That can influence Christians to express their faith with an over-emphasis on the here and now. They even see other people, lost people, purely in terms of this life. Our love for others becomes taken up with giving to the needy rather than sharing the gospel. We fixate on climate change and saving the planet more than the message of the cross. Of course, caring for the needy and being concerned about global warming have a place, but those things are ultimately temporary issues. The gospel brings forgiveness and eternal life. We can lose that focus.

Prayer takes a back seat. Many people see it as more necessary to check their phone or their iPad before checking in with God each day. They spend more time in the shower in the morning than they do with the Lord. And if you stood back and asked what the focus of their agenda is, you would rapidly come to the conclusion that it was their own comfort or interests. This is immaturity.

Church becomes a social rather than a spiritual event. There's no dispute that it's great to have friends at church. We are called to love one another. But should seeing friends at church actually mean more to us than God Himself? This is juvenile Christianity.

Worship becomes a tick-box exercise. It frequently fails to be a matter of the heart. We 'do church'. Churches begin to play to what people enjoy rather than what pleases God. We produce beautiful sermons and choreographed services. But no tears are shed over sin; no heart is touched. We have simply checked the box for Sunday. This is immaturity.

WHAT GOD'S CHURCHES NEED

Instead of this lackadaisical approach we need to prioritise Christ, the gospel and the building of His kingdom. Let me give some very practical and obvious examples of how mature Christians do this.

Let's look at your diary. How do you use it for Christ? I knew of a husband and wife who, when they got their diaries for the New Year, went through the whole and, before marking anything else, blocked out Sundays and Thursday evenings. These were the times that their church met for worship and for prayer. Now they weren't totally inflexible on that. But it was the base, the bottom line, from which they started each year.

Let's look at where you live. Most churches would be really helped by people in the congregation living in the area (walking distance) of where the church meets. When that happens, it means we are on hand to help with jobs. It helps our witness. It is simple to leaflet the houses. It is easy to invite our neighbours to church because it is just down the road. But so often Christians think otherwise. 'The houses in the area around the church are not as nice as I would like. And anyway we need to live five miles away so we can get our children into that nice school.' What is really controlling such decisions? Whatever it is, it is not the priority of spreading the gospel.

We could push this a little further. People in Britain have a great need to hear the gospel. Many small gospel churches across the country are crying out for help. Ask yourself, 'Could I, with the blessing of my church, move to another place in order to help a struggling congregation?' To move house is a big matter. But is it bigger than the needs of Christ's cause?

I know there are other factors in these matters concerning family and elderly parents who require looking after, etc. But in the final analysis, our decision-making concerning such practical issues can often be quite worldly and immature. It is time to grow up. Either we believe that Christ is Lord, and His gospel is the most important thing in the world, or we don't. It's time to do away with this jumble of priorities and muddle of ideas – a mind like a teenager's bedroom. It's time to say, 'No. I'm no longer going to just jog along and hang loose. I'm going to follow in the footsteps of Paul and the Philippians with the priority of the gospel.'

HOW CAN WE MAKE PROGRESS?

What is our commitment? What kind of priority does the Lord actually have for me? Every Christian needs to review their lives now and then with such questions in mind. Here are some particular items to think about.

We need to pray. In ourselves we easily give in to the ways of the world. It was God who brought us to commit ourselves to Christ. He is the one who began the good work in us (1:6), and only He can maintain that good work. So we need to pray that He will continue that good work. The Lord Jesus was concerned about the salt losing its saltiness (Luke 14:34). That can happen to us as Christians over time if we are not careful. Pray that the Lord will work to deepen our engagement with Christ and stir up our zeal. We need to rededicate ourselves and pray that the Lord will deliver us from being superficial.

In this section of Philippians, Paul himself, as a Christian leader, has set *the example of commitment*. Leaders must do this. Obviously, they must teach from Scripture commitment to Christ and the gospel. Such teaching is good. But church leaders must challenge people by their lives too (4:9). We do not believe in brute force and leaders pushing their people around. Christians must come to set priorities and make sacrificial decisions for themselves. So what will help them in this? It is often leaders who set a good example. Does the church leadership really put itself out for Christ's cause? Or has it actually become quite a comfortable life? Does your church leadership take a lead in the difficult and daunting task of sharing the gospel with other people? Are they like Paul?

In our verses, the individuals which made up the church in Philippi showed their commitment to Christ and the spread of the gospel by *the support they gave to Paul.* God has gifted particular individuals to be evangelists and preachers of His Word. If we truly prioritise Jesus in our lives, we will get behind these men and we will get behind gospel initiatives. Yes, we will take whatever opportunities arise for ourselves to share the good news with friends, neighbours and colleagues. But mainly we will support – through prayer, encouragement and finance – those whom God thrusts into the forefront of evangelism. We will be serious about prayer and giving to mission.

Do we find our joy in the spread of the gospel? There is so much thankfulness and joy in this opening chapter of Philippians (vv. 3, 8, 18, 25, 26). But it is joy that flows out of Christ and the spread of the gospel being the biggest thing in life. Paul finds thankfulness welling up in him as he hears of the gospel spreading and Christians making progress. Is that the greatest source of joy in your life? If it is, it shows where your heart is. It shows a deep commitment to Christ and His work. If that's not where our true joy is found, then where is it found? Where our hearts are located says a great deal about us. A mature Christian finds his or her joy in Christ, His gospel and His people.

Again, *when it comes to choosing leaders for churches*, Paul says later in Philippians that it is those who give their all and are prepared to take risks for the gospel that the church should honour, when he commends Epaphroditus (2:29). In the current climate, our churches tend to be a little too comfortable for our own good. There is often a disquieting correlation between who is in the church leadership and who has the highest salaries in the congregation. To appoint as leaders those who have not made it in their careers, but who have sacrificed career opportunities because they are out and out for the gospel, would do us no harm. It would probably do us a lot of good. We need leaders who set the gospel priority. These are the role models that churches need in order to 'come of age' and grow up.

Grown-up Christians press on to up their game when it comes to prioritising the gospel. Those who are immature are always ducking in and out of responsibilities. But let's take our priority seriously. It's the adult thing to do.

Chapter 3

The Mature Church's Community

Many young students during the 1960s were enamoured with the songs of the Canadian poet and writer, Leonard Cohen. His plaintive love songs for lonely hearts in a bleak secular age chimed in with the adolescent outlook in the era of 'free love' and were thought extremely cool.

Cohen had a long-term relationship with Marianne Ihlen, a young Norwegian woman who became the inspiration for many of his lyrics. One of his most famous songs was 'So long Marianne'. Marianne had a young son, Axel, by a previous relationship and Cohen tried to help. In between times on tour or in New York, he lived together with them on the Greek island of Hydra, often as both he and Marianne pursued relationships with other people.

And amid the chaotic, non-committed love affair it was the child who had the worst of it. With no stability he was deeply disturbed and later ended up in an institution. One recent article on the Cohen–Ihlen liaison makes these telling remarks: 'Life on the island was an idyll, but one that cursed many who lived it.

CHURCH FOR GROWN UPS

When adults pursue their second childhood, it's their children who suffer.'[1]

Society today encourages us to live in a perpetual 'second childhood'. Hanging loose to relationships is the way of the adolescent. To be committed shuts down options and restricts freedom for the person eager to try new experiences. But just as that attitude wrecks children and families via lack of emotional security, so lack of commitment to God's people debilitates churches. Mature churches know something of commitment to gospel community.

With this in mind we now look at Philippians 1:27–2:30:

> *Whatever happens, conduct yourselves in a manner worthy of the gospel of Christ. Then, whether I come and see you or only hear about you in my absence, I will know that you stand firm in the one Spirit, striving together as one for the faith of the gospel without being frightened in any way by those who oppose you. This is a sign to them that they will be destroyed, but that you will be saved—and that by God. For it has been granted to you on behalf of Christ not only to believe in him, but also to suffer for him, since you are going through the same struggle you saw I had, and now hear that I still have.*
>
> *Therefore if you have any encouragement from being united with Christ, if any comfort from his love, if any common sharing in the Spirit, if any tenderness and compassion, then make my joy complete by being like-minded, having the same love, being one in spirit and of one mind. Do nothing out of selfish ambition or vain conceit. Rather, in humility value others above yourselves, not looking to your own interests but each of you to the interests of the others.*
>
> *In your relationships with one another, have the same mind-set as Christ Jesus:*
>
> *Who, being in very nature God,*
> *did not consider equality with God something to be used to his*

1   Mick Brown, *The Week*, 3/8/2019, p. 53.

own advantage;
rather, he made himself nothing
by taking the very nature of a servant,
being made in human likeness.
And being found in appearance as a man,
he humbled himself
by becoming obedient to death—
even death on a cross!
Therefore God exalted him to the highest place
and gave him the name that is above every name,
that at the name of Jesus every knee should bow,
in heaven and on earth and under the earth,
and every tongue acknowledge that Jesus Christ is Lord,
to the glory of God the Father.

Therefore, my dear friends, as you have always obeyed—not only in my presence, but now much more in my absence—continue to work out your salvation with fear and trembling, for it is God who works in you to will and to act in order to fulfil his good purpose. Do everything without grumbling or arguing, so that you may become blameless and pure, 'children of God without fault in a warped and crooked generation.' Then you will shine among them like stars in the sky as you hold firmly to the word of life. And then I will be able to boast on the day of Christ that I did not run or labour in vain. But even if I am being poured out like a drink offering on the sacrifice and service coming from your faith, I am glad and rejoice with all of you. So you too should be glad and rejoice with me.

I hope in the Lord Jesus to send Timothy to you soon, that I also may be cheered when I receive news about you. I have no one else like him, who will show genuine concern for your welfare. For everyone looks out for their own interests, not those of Jesus Christ. But you know that Timothy has proved himself, because as a son with his father he has served with me in the work of the gospel. I hope, therefore, to send him as soon as I see how things go with me. And I am confident in the Lord that I myself will come soon.

> *But I think it is necessary to send back to you Epaphroditus, my brother, co-worker and fellow soldier, who is also your messenger, whom you sent to take care of my needs. For he longs for all of you and is distressed because you heard he was ill. Indeed he was ill, and almost died. But God had mercy on him, and not on him only but also on me, to spare me sorrow upon sorrow. Therefore I am all the more eager to send him, so that when you see him again you may be glad and I may have less anxiety. So then, welcome him in the Lord with great joy, and honor people like him, because he almost died for the work of Christ. He risked his life to make up for the help you yourselves could not give me.*

This section includes the famous passage describing the humility and exaltation of our Lord Jesus Christ with Paul calling us to follow Christ's example of servanthood. But this comes in the context of a call to unity in the church. It is basically an exhortation to be deeply at one. Paul asks the members of the church in Philippi to 'make my joy complete by being like-minded, having the same love, being one in spirit and of one mind' (2:2). And notice the context of that call for the church to work together as a team is again gospel-centred. It is that they may 'stand firm in one spirit, contending as one man for the faith of the gospel' (1:27). The Philippians are to work together without complaining or arguing, as they 'hold firmly the word of life' (2:16). The grown-up church pulls together as a gospel community.

GREATER THAN THE SUM OF THE PARTS

There are collections of things which, when they are brought together in a certain way, have a power that is greater than the sum total of the separate parts.

Take all the parts of an electric battery. There is an anode and a cathode and an electrolyte of some kind. In the early days these were rods of copper and zinc and the electrolyte was sulphuric acid. Separately, none of them would make light. But put them together in a particular way and, lo and behold, there is electricity, the current flows, you have a battery – a power source. You produce electricity, and it can power a lightbulb or even a computer. When the components come together in a certain way, something new happens that wasn't there before.

Or think about all the components of an old-fashioned mechanical alarm clock: cogs and wheels and springs and metallic hands. Separately they are only a pile of junk. But fix them together appropriately and they can tell the time! They have the ability to get someone out of bed! They have an ability together which outstrips the sum of what they could do separately.

If you merely throw the components of a battery together any-how, they won't produce electricity. If you only pile the bits of an alarm clock together, they won't work. And if a bunch of less than perfect Christians come together in any old way, with any old attitudes, they won't glorify Christ. They won't help each other or promote the gospel (1:27). But if they come together in the right way, it's all very different.

How we come together

What is the way that Christians need to relate to each other as the church? Paul's answer to that question is that we have to come together following the example of Christ: 'have the same mindset as Christ Jesus...' (2:5). This is the key which unlocks the door to a church being more than just a collection of religious people.

- We are to put away conceit (2:3-4). Pride is the characteristic of the devil and wreaks havoc in any church. So put it aside.
- We are to put aside our rights, just as Jesus did to humble Himself (2:6-7). By rights, where should you and I be? I'll tell you – in outer darkness. But God has graciously saved

us and not given us our rights! So let's stop all that insisting on them.

- We should become like servants (2:7-8). Jesus made Himself a slave, even to the extent of dying for us on the cross. And if in Christ, God can humble Himself to become a servant, who are we to think that it is below us to become servants of each other?

A mature, grown-up church 'gets' this. This way of doing things captures their imagination. It touches their hearts. They see it and do their best to apply it. A mature, grown-up church is a church where this Christlike attitude of servanthood is both prized and practiced – even when things are difficult. In a mature church, this becomes the routine way of relating to one another.

Of course, this is a challenge to sinners like us. Dawson Trotman, the founder of The Navigators, a Christian organisation which has done great work in encouraging Christians to memorise Scripture and dig deeper into the Bible, summed it up well. He said: 'You don't really know if you have a servant heart until someone treats you like one!' We can feel belittled. When we get treated like a servant, we can feel unappreciated. But the people of a mature church rise to such challenges and meet them with humility.

What is the worst job you can think of for the church? Perhaps it is cleaning the church toilets. Are you up for doing that? I know of one unsung hero who did this cheerfully and had the nickname 'The Lord of the Rims'! The Lord was pleased to be a servant. That's maturity. That's being like Jesus.

Because we are less than perfect Christians, we can irritate each other. Many churches fracture over personal conflicts. But the kind, humble, servant attitude, which we find in Philippians 2, inspired by the example of Jesus, makes for a united church.

And that unity has power to reach across the boundaries of race, wealth, gender and age. It produces true Christian community. It makes for a good team which is 'striving together as one for the faith of the gospel' (1:27).

How mature is your church? Here is how you know. Look at Philippians 2. What is taught there is how you gauge the maturity of a church. You do not gauge it by its size. You do not gauge it by the quality of its music, or even of its preacher. You do not gauge it by how well organised and efficient it is. The measure of a church is how much it is like Jesus. It is about humility, love and service in Christ. And these things lead to loving community and unity. This is the measure of how grown-up we are spiritually.

ROADBLOCKS TO UNITY

What are the obstacles to such gospel community? We have already flagged up some of them. As Paul points out in the passage, there is also our own pride and selfishness.

- There is selfish ambition and vain conceit (2:3). There is the natural sinful tendency to think of ourselves and our own comforts first and ignore the needs of others.
- There is that desire for prominence. Jesus spoke of the tendency which is in all of us to 'pick the places of honour at the table' (Luke 14:7).
- The apostle John knew the bad influence a man named Diotrephes, 'who loves to be first', was having in the churches of his day (3 John 9).
- Paul was aware of our tendency to become puffed up with our own importance, e.g., 1 Timothy 3:6, which speaks of the possibility of conceited elders.

We know that all this is not Christlike behaviour. Our pride, for example, can hurt others, causing anger and division. These things we have to fight daily as individuals and as a church.

But there can be more subtle things at work these days to undermine true community. Let's identify a couple.

HOMOGENEOUS PEOPLE GROUPS?

Some churches have swallowed the idea of the target audience. They go after a 'niche market'. They pursue the idea that people like to be with people like themselves. For example, 'Young couples attract other young couples – so let's concentrate on young couples,' they say to themselves. This is adopted as a church strategy. And it becomes almost a 'gospel argument' to ignore the New Testament's emphasis on the unity of the church across all ages and social boundaries.

This strategy has picked up on ideas from the world of business. To market a product, firms are told that they need to aim at a specific audience and tailor things specifically to appeal to that group of people. This is a way to improve your business.

So churches shape services or organise events in order to attract a particular group of people – often it's young people, but not always. Now, there is a balance here. We must not totally exclude the idea of outreach to specific groups. Sometimes it is not bad to have a men's breakfast or a women's craft evening, or a Chinese Bible study, etc. But there has been a trend in many larger churches to have separate congregations for particular sections of people. They might have a youth service in the evening and a family service in the morning. But they can end up with two different congregations which never interact. The unity is not there.

I know an older man who was a member of a large congregation in London and decided to go along to the evening service. He found himself being challenged by the minister. 'What are you doing here?' he was asked, 'this is a youth service for people under thirty.' The implication was that he was not really welcome, and he felt it.

We must ask ourselves how that squares with Philippians 2. It doesn't. By such strategies young people are unconsciously being taught to put their own interests and the interests of their own peer group before the needs of others. It has the wrong outlook. It smells bad.

At the other end of the spectrum, there may be a church of older people who insist on an ancient Bible version and using hymns written before the twentieth century because this is what *they* like. It comes across as a total rejection of the twenty-first century and of its children. The underlying message is, 'we only want people like us in our church'. The whole idea of give and take and thinking of others as 'better than yourselves' is lost (2:3). People are ignored instead of standing together for the cause of the gospel.

JESUS IS LORD

But Christianity says that Christ is Lord of all – old and young, rich and poor, men and women, native born or foreign – whatever. The good news is for all. Christ's gospel is more important than our personal likes and dislikes. If that fact is never seen in our churches we actually fail to show who Jesus really is. In other words, if that gospel oneness is muted or hardly ever demonstrated in the church, you have an immature church. In a world torn apart by racial tensions, does it really help to have 'black churches' and 'white churches'?

The point is that the world can produce a unity and community of people all of the same age or who all like the same things. It can bring together sports fanatics at World Cups and Olympic Games. It can bring together music lovers at gigs and concerts. It can bring together drinkers at beer festivals. It can bring together bikers at rallies. But this is not the across-the-board unity of the Spirit. This is not a demonstration of the Lordship of Christ over all.

It is when the world sees a unity and happy community made up of those who do not naturally fit together that it sits up and takes notice, because it knows something unusual is happening. In the New Testament times the great social divide was between Jews and Gentiles. So when Jews and Gentiles came together in the church it was seen as something astonishing. God was obviously at work. It is a church where there is unity and love between rich and poor, black and white, left-wingers and right-wingers, old and young, that shows a real witness for Christ. This church has a power greater than the sum of its parts. Jesus prayed for His people 'that all of them may be one, Father, just as you are in me and I am in you. May they also be in us that the world may believe that you sent me' (John 17:21).

CHURCHES LIKE SUPERMARKETS?

Another obstacle to unity in the church can be its size. We thank God when churches grow. To see people converted to Christ and the church getting bigger is a great joy. However, as a church grows it should really begin to think about how it can plant other churches in nearby communities. But sometimes that doesn't happen, and the church really becomes too big for its own good. The sense of community is lost.

On too many occasions in larger congregations I have heard stories of Christians greeting those they thought were visitors or new to the area only to find that people say, 'Actually I've been coming to this church for the past six months.' Such churches no longer feel like a body or a family where every member is important. Sundays have more the ethos of a concert where people come to enjoy the 'performance' – or come over more like a supermarket where congregants drive in to stock up on spiritual supplies from the services and then drive off again until the following Lord's Day.

Often, larger churches try to address the fellowship side of church by setting up small groups and home meetings – which have their place. But people do not share and love one another across the whole congregation because they just don't know each other. Sometimes churches grow like this through sheer laziness. Lazy Christians join large churches because there are so many people that they are not likely to be asked to do too much. Lazy leaderships tell themselves that it would be a great deal of trouble to plant a new congregation and if 'it ain't broke – don't fix it'.

But the kind of servant-hearted unity and depth of togetherness which Paul has in mind in Philippians 2 is largely lost. Very often, instead of the whole church contending as one man for the gospel and shining as stars in a crooked world with everybody involved in loving service, the majority of members of large churches simply 'pay their subs' and leave the work to the zealous few and the salaried staff. They are passengers, not those who pull together. Big it may be. Spiritually mature it ain't!

So the big church, as an ideal, needs some rethinking.

How can we make progress?

What are some practical, hands-on ways to bring a church together in community?

First, we must experience the love of God towards us in the gospel. Paul speaks of being encouraged by 'being united with Christ' and of being 'comforted' by His love (2:1). He reminds us of knowing the life of the Holy Spirit in our hearts, and of enjoying the tenderness and compassion of the Lord. It is from such experiences that we will learn to be kind to others. As Christians we sometimes fall into sin, but we seek God and tenderly He forgives us. 'Well,' says Paul, 'remember that and turn that experience into tenderness towards others.' 'You didn't deserve His forgiveness,' Paul is implying, 'but He was gracious to you. So be gracious to others.' There may have been times when we have been very worried or downcast. But as you have prayed the Lord has lifted you up. Remember how the Lord has been kind to you and so be kind to others. In such ways we make progress in treating others in the right way.

Second, we must stop complaining (2:14). A critical spirit is not 'the gift of discernment' as I have heard some people claim when trying to justify their unhelpful attitudes. A critical spirit often comes back to being self-seeking. A true gift of discernment sees the problems but tries to humbly point them out and the way forward in a way that builds up and does not knock down. Our first thought should be to encourage and, then, when there may be problems which need confronting, others will find it easier to respond well, knowing that you are a person who honestly loves the church and desires to see it prosper.

Third, if we really do want to 'look...to the interests of others' a fruitful weekly exercise is this: Before you go to church consider the different people in the church, pray for them and think through what you might be able to say to encourage them. It may be that they have done something recently for which you can thank them and say how much you appreciated what they did. It may be that they are going through a difficult time and you can find a promise from God's Word which they might find uplifting. They might find help by you asking if you can pray for them. Care for others was what made Paul's young lieutenant Timothy an outstanding helper (2:20).

Fourth, be careful how you think about services. A church must do whatever it can to avoid people in the congregation thinking of themselves as an audience and those on the platform as 'performers'. (We have all cringed at the immature 'wanna-be' singer who leads the music group, treating a service as if it is their big opportunity on *Britain's Got Talent*.)[2] The preacher and the musicians are there to serve, not to perform. Our true audience of everyone in church – leaders and congregation – is the God who looks on our hearts. He is looking for servants, not superstars.

Fifth, leaders have to teach Christlike service. Leaders must teach Philippians 2. But then having taught it, leaders, do not be above getting your hands dirty yourself in works of service, humbling yourself. Yes, I know that your preaching must come first, but not in a way that fails to set an example. In Philippians 2:19-30 we are introduced to two church leaders who set great examples. Of Timothy, Paul writes: 'I have no-one else like him, who takes a genuine interest in your welfare,' and 'as a son with his father he has served with me in the work of the gospel' (2:20, 22). Then we are introduced to Epaphroditus who 'almost died for the work of Christ, risking his life to make up for the help you could not give me' (2:30). We have made the point before, but it is worth repeating: leaders who practice what they preach in service are a real inspiration and show the church the way to maturity.

Sixth, food often seems to have been an important part of the early church. Eating together as a fellowship gives lots of opportunity to begin to serve, to wait at the table as Jesus did

---

2   I wonder what would happen if music groups were positioned at the back of the church instead of at the front? It might save us from the 'performance' syndrome. But maybe there would be issues with timing between musicians and congregation.

(John 13:14). And that attitude of service can overflow into other aspects of church life.

Seventh, a church away day with some teaching and some purposeful fun can often bring a new spirit of acceptance and enjoyment of being with one another to a congregation.

WHY DO WE NEED THIS GOSPEL COMMUNITY?

There are many reasons why oneness across the congregation is something to be desired and highly prized – not least because such unity and love is a sign to the principalities and powers of the victory of Christ and the 'manifold wisdom of God' (Eph. 3:10).

But the reason which Paul flags up here in Philippians is that unity is needed because if the church is truly spreading the gospel and contending in the public arena for Christ, it will face opposition. And there might be times when the opposition is so stiff that you will be tempted to be frightened. A church will be strong in the face of opposition if its people stand together with a deep care for one another (1:28-30). This is becoming of great relevance to us now. It seems that in the twenty-first century, evangelical faith is facing increasingly aggressive opposition from our society. We will touch on this again later. The great forces of 'inclusiveness', political correctness, the liberal media and the power of Islam are ranged against us. We need to be committed to each other in order to encourage each other and stay strong for Christ.

Earlier, I used the illustrations of the bits of a battery or the bits of an alarm clock. If they are put together in a certain way, they are capable of things they could never do separately. Is there such extra power in the church? I believe there is. It is the power of God. We are to be careful to come together with Christlike humility and love, because God is at work among us (2:12-

13). Where Christians love and serve each other, God's Spirit works powerfully. The Psalmist had it right: 'How good and how pleasant it is when brothers live together in unity...for there the Lord bestows his blessing' (Ps. 133). But churches can grieve the Spirit through mistreating and hurting one another. Churches can lose their power and become mere hollow shells. But as we follow the way of Christ, we will inevitably see more of the power of God. We will indeed 'shine like stars in the universe' (2:15).

Church for grown-ups? It is about the quality of love, the priority of the gospel and servant community.

Chapter 4

The Mature Church's **Integrity**

When I was a young boy our family was invited to go for a holiday to stay with a naval officer's family based on the Gare Loch in Scotland. He was an officer on a submarine support ship (*HMS Adamant*). This was immensely exciting for me for a number of reasons. It was the first time we had ever been to Scotland. As we travelled from Heathrow to Glasgow it was the first time I had ever flown in an aeroplane. And it was going to be great to be shown a little of a naval base supporting the British nuclear submarine fleet on the Clyde.

But the trouble was, my teenaged sister came with us. She had just discovered the love of her life (or so she thought). And she would have to leave him behind for a whole week. Over-whelmed by her adolescent emotions, she was lovelorn, moody, awkward and irritable and generally made it a very difficult time for the whole family. All this cast a cloud over the whole experience. Don't worry, all these years later, I have forgiven her – just!

She was adolescent and immature. To live on our feelings, to be ruled by changing emotions, is a mark of immaturity. It is okay to go through that emotional phase as a teenager; everyone does. It is normal. But it is a phase you leave behind, and you learn to control your emotions without them controlling you, and you grow up. You have to learn to live in the real world, according to the way things truly are.

However, in the last forty years or so we have been, as we have said, under the growing influence of secularism and its idolisation of youth. Our whole Western culture has come to be re-orientated towards emotion and an emotional agenda for life. And the church has been affected.

This great shift[1] has been away from an outlook on life where behaviour was governed by truth and error / right and wrong seen as realities outside of ourselves – in other words a moral / reasoned culture. We have been brought into a culture of *pathos,* of feeling as opposed to reason. Whereas good and bad used to be defined in terms of external standards of right and wrong, they are now much more defined in terms of inward and changeable feelings. Good is what makes you feel good. Bad is what makes someone feel bad.

We can see this shift in all kinds of ways; from those unfortunate TV interviews where the only question the reporter is able to come up with seems to be 'how did you feel about that?' to what has at times been the undermining of an entire working school examination system because no one should be made to feel that they have failed. Melanie Phillips' book, *All Must Have Prizes,*[2] is one of the many which explains what has happened.

---

1   This shift goes hand in hand with a postmodern outlook.

2   *All Must Have Prizes*, by Melanie Phillips (Little Brown, 1996).

THE GOSPEL AND 'FEEL GOOD'

We have shifted from a moral culture to what sociologists call an emotional or 'therapy culture'. Our world is secular. We don't believe in God. There are no absolutes of morality. People believe there is no greater purpose in life than to 'have a good time'. So they just concentrate on making themselves feel good and making other people feel good about themselves. And much of the church, whether consciously or unconsciously, has bought into this way of thinking in a big way. But in biblical terms the focus on feelings tends to make us immature.

Because the Bible does believe in God and does believe in right and wrong, and with the whole of the gospel being predicated upon God's holiness and the subsequent moral framework of our lives, to be focused on feelings won't do. Before we can feel good, we need our sins (our objective moral failure) forgiven through the redemption that is in Christ.

Buying into therapy culture is inviting to Christians because, superficially at least, it looks so caring and loving. It aims first and foremost at making people 'feel better'. But it is founded on a worldview which is not biblical. And when it comes to Christians it actually retards or even reverses their growth to spiritual maturity in a number of ways.

This is the context we need to draw on as we look at the next mark of a mature church. We have to look at a church's fidelity regarding God's truth. Does a church have integrity regarding the gospel?

In this chapter we first look at gospel integrity as shown in Philippians 3:1–4:1:

> *Further, my brothers and sisters, rejoice in the Lord! It is no trouble for me to write the same things to you again, and it is a safeguard for you.*

Watch out for those dogs, those evildoers, those mutilators of the flesh. For it is we who are the circumcision, we who serve God by his Spirit, who boast in Christ Jesus, and who put no confidence in the flesh—though I myself have reasons for such confidence.

If someone else thinks they have reasons to put confidence in the flesh, I have more: circumcised on the eighth day, of the people of Israel, of the tribe of Benjamin, a Hebrew of Hebrews; in regard to the law, a Pharisee; as for zeal, persecuting the church; as for righteousness based on the law, faultless.

But whatever were gains to me I now consider loss for the sake of Christ. What is more, I consider everything a loss because of the surpassing worth of knowing Christ Jesus my Lord, for whose sake I have lost all things. I consider them garbage, that I may gain Christ and be found in him, not having a righteousness of my own that comes from the law, but that which is through faith in Christ—the righteousness that comes from God on the basis of faith. I want to know Christ—yes, to know the power of his resurrection and participation in his sufferings, becoming like him in his death, and so, somehow, attaining to the resurrection from the dead.

Not that I have already obtained all this, or have already arrived at my goal, but I press on to take hold of that for which Christ Jesus took hold of me. Brothers and sisters, I do not consider myself yet to have taken hold of it. But one thing I do: Forgetting what is behind and straining toward what is ahead, I press on toward the goal to win the prize for which God has called me heavenward in Christ Jesus.

All of us, then, who are mature should take such a view of things. And if on some point you think differently, that too God will make clear to you. Only let us live up to what we have already attained. Join together in following my example, brothers and sisters, and just as you have us as a model, keep your eyes on those who live as we do. For, as I have often told you before and now tell you again even with tears, many live as enemies of the cross of Christ. Their destiny is destruction, their god is their stomach, and their glory is in their shame. Their mind is set on earthly things. But our citizenship is in heaven. And we eagerly await a Saviour from there, the Lord Jesus Christ, who, by the power that

> *enables him to bring everything under his control, will transform our lowly bodies so that they will be like his glorious body. Therefore, my brothers and sisters, you whom I love and long for, my joy and crown, stand firm in the Lord in this way, dear friends!*

These verses form the close of a section which is about standing firm for the gospel. It begins in 1:27 where Paul encourages the Philippians to conduct themselves in a way worthy of the gospel and says this will lead them to 'stand firm in one spirit'. It ends at 4:1 which looks back over what he has written and concludes with 'that is how you should stand firm in the Lord, dear friends.'

You stand firm, first of all, as chapter 2 says, by standing together, in unity, with a Christlike attitude to one another, holding out the gospel. But secondly, and equally importantly, you stand firm by embracing and defending the truth of the gospel with integrity and without compromise.

In chapter 3 Paul commends the gospel and warns against error. The gospel is concerned with the facts of what has happened in history in the life, death and resurrection of Jesus, and what God says these facts mean. The Philippians must uphold apostolic truth despite repeated attacks from false teachers. This is vital. Hence Paul begins by saying, 'It is no trouble for me to write the same things to you again, and it is a safeguard for you. Watch out for those dogs, those men who do evil...' (3:1b, 2a).

It might be helpful to see this chapter through the lens of 'the heresies of the three Joes'. Here we meet ordinary Joe, holy Joe and sloppy Joe, all of whom will lead us astray from the truth of the gospel if we are not careful.

ORDINARY JOE

First, Paul tells us that the gospel is not the religion of the *Ordinary Joe* (3:2-11). If you ask ordinary Joe – sometimes referred to as 'the man in the street' – what the gospel is, he is likely to come up with an answer similar to that of the Pharisees.

Theologically, it is a form of semi-Pelagianism. Ordinary Joe says, 'be good, do your best, and with a bit of help from God, hopefully you will be good enough for heaven.'[3] But Paul emphatically denies that acceptance with God depends even one iota on his own attainments. If it did, how could you ever know if you had done enough? That leaves someone forever anxious and uncertain. And if you did think you had done enough, wouldn't you legitimately be able to boast and think yourself better than other people? After all, you had done something to attain heaven that other people have not. Then what kind of person would you be? You would become proud and priggish and put more people off the gospel than attract them to it. In contrast to such pride, Paul counts all that belongs to him, in and of himself, as rubbish (v. 8).

The good news is that acceptance with God is a totally free gift to be received through faith in Christ. Paul looks only to Jesus: 'and to be found in him, not having a righteousness of my own that comes from the law, but that which is through faith in Christ – the righteousness that comes from God and is by faith' (v. 9). Ordinary Joe thinks in terms of measuring up by our own efforts at goodness. But Paul looks to a righteousness that is not his own but is instead the free gift of God. So beware of ordinary Joe! He will rob you of the gospel and of the humble happiness which boasts only of God and rejoices in Christ alone (v. 1).

It was the rediscovery of this gospel of grace, salvation as a free gift, which was the driving force of the Reformation and set the church free after centuries of fear and spiritual bondage. It is never to be surrendered.

---

3   Those who were enamoured by The New Perspective, a decade or so ago, were inadvertently trying to lead us back into this heresy.

HOLY JOE

Second, Paul tells us that the gospel does not mean perfection in this life (3:12-16). Perfectionism is a heresy. It is not the gospel. From time to time idiots arise within the church who teach that we can become perfect Christians here and now. I call them the *Holy Joes*. They are false teachers.

They teach there is some second blessing, or some extra gigantic effort of dedication, which will enable you to cross the line and make you all you could wish to be as a Christian. You become a 'super-Christian' on a separate plane from others. This teaching wreaks havoc in a church. It swells some people with pride because they think they have made it, and it plunges others into despair because they think they have not. It divides churches.

But Paul specifically repudiates the Holy Joes. He has told of his yearning to be like Christ (vv. 10-11), but then quickly adds: 'Not that I have already obtained all this, or have been made perfect, but I press on to take hold of that for which Christ Jesus took hold of me. Brothers, I do not consider myself yet to have taken hold of it. But one thing I do: Forgetting what is behind and straining forward towards what is ahead I press on towards the goal to win the prize for which God called me heavenward in Christ Jesus' (vv. 12-14). The present life for the Christian is one of aspiration, not of consummation. Nevertheless we keep the consummation very much in mind. However, that consummation is not here, but in heaven. Hence Paul presses on heavenwards. So Holy Joe meets his nemesis in the apostle Paul.

Giving in to Holy Joe's ideas, in their various forms, always causes division and hurt in the church. We cease to be a band of brothers and sisters. We become instead a company of 'haves' and 'have-nots'. This false path of perfectionism is to be resisted at all costs.

SLOPPY JOE

But then thirdly, in contrast to the Holy Joes there are the *Sloppy Joes* (vv. 17-21).[4] They call themselves Christians but show no evidence of living for God or following in Christ's footsteps. They simply say, 'If Jesus dealt with my sin, it doesn't matter how I live.' They turn up at church but live a sloppy, ungodly life. But Paul warns the Philippians away from the Sloppy Joes.

The gospel not only puts us right with God, it also changes us as people. The gospel is 'the truth that leads to godliness' (Titus 1:1). Paul warns the Philippians away from Sloppy Joe because he is not living in line with the gospel which calls us to heaven and its way of life. And if they allow him houseroom, Sloppy Joe's ways will rub off on them and spoil the church. 'For, as I have often told you before and now say again even with tears, many live as enemies of the cross of Christ.... Their mind is on earthly things. But our citizenship is in heaven...' (vv. 18-20).

Sloppy Joe denies the reality of the new birth through faith in Jesus. He denies that the Holy Spirit changes lives or makes a difference to us. He doesn't care that God's aim is to have a holy people for Himself.

Christians are seeking to become like Jesus. We are not what we would like to be. We are not yet what we shall be. But we are not what we used to be. Sloppy Joe is to be challenged, not embraced.

So here Paul is telling us to beware of aberrations from the gospel, if we are to carry on making progress in Christ and

---

4   A 'Sloppy Joe' is a kind of hamburger sandwich containing ground beef or pork and onions – but we use it here as the name of a careless, lazy or sloppy person.

become mature. And it is worth noting that he indicates that he has addressed these things before in his interaction with the Philippians (vv. 1, 18). Here he writes about them 'again' (v. 1). Ordinary Joe, Holy Joe and Sloppy Joe are always hanging around trying to gain entrance and acceptance in the church and in our lives. We may have thrown them out once, but then we open the door and there they are hoping to gain re-admittance and so wreck our Christian lives and churches. We have to fight them off again and again.

NON-NEGOTIABLE DOCTRINE

Paul's concern with opposing these poisonous mutations of the gospel is patently rooted in Christian doctrine. The apostolic gospel is part and parcel with non-negotiable Biblical truth on such subjects as God, sin, Christ, the cross, faith and heaven.

God is the living God who created all things and has revealed Himself reliably in the Bible and through His Son, Jesus Christ. He is a holy God before whom even the angels veil their faces. Sin is any deviation from the requirements of God's holiness. We, as human beings, are a fallen race, with sin endemic in us and that imprisons us. This is why it is impossible for us to contribute in any way to our own redemption. Whatever we touch will be tainted. If we are to be restored to a relationship with God, only He can do it. The good news is of grace, not legalistic self-help. God in His mercy sent His Son, the Lord Jesus Christ, who is both God and man, in one person and without sin. He died on the cross in obedience to God His Father as our substitute, to pay for our sins and make us right with God. This restoration to God comes as we repent and are united to Christ by faith. It is Christ who opens the door to eternal life and heaven for sinners, and for them to enjoy a new heaven and earth when He returns in glory.

These basic doctrines lay behind Paul's exhortations in this chapter and will be cherished and prized by all mature Christians and mature churches.

Standing back a moment – leaving aside the specifics – what has been Paul's concern in chapter 3? It has been a concern for the truth of the gospel but also for having integrity about living in the light of it. His concern is with doctrine and with doctrine lived out – without anxiety like ordinary Joe; without pride like holy Joe; and without carelessness like sloppy Joe.

WHY WE HANG LOOSE TO DOCTRINE

Therefore, we need to think about the obstacles which emerge in the modern world to our being clear about doctrine and what we believe.

The first obstacle comes from history. There have been too many times in the past when churches divided in acrimonious ways over doctrinal differences. Often these involved secondary matters, like baptism or church government. We scratch our heads at the multitude of denominations and wonder whether it was all really necessary. It doesn't seem to have done any good for the credibility of Christianity in the eyes of the onlooking world. In the minds of many Christians this consequence tends to give doctrine *per se* a bad press and so we hang loose to it.

The second obstacle emerges from the atmosphere of our therapy culture. It is an emotional objection. Driven by the feel-good society around us, many churches renege on truth, at least to the extent, that unlike Paul, they are not prepared to have a confrontation about it. Confrontation doesn't feel very nice. A battle can be bloody. So with increasing frequency nowadays you hear people say things like, 'Look, let's not bicker about what we believe. It is only doctrine. We should focus instead on loving one another and how we live. Let's set aside our disagreements over creeds and dogmas and instead just show the love of Christ.' But when we hear words like that, we don't hear the apostle Paul speaking, or Jesus speaking; we hear our therapy culture speaking. Remember, Paul wants us to 'stand firm' on the gospel (4:1). Otherwise we are immature.

The third obstacle, forming the basis for the first, is postmodernism. This is a more intellectual objection. The 'modernism' of the Enlightenment believed in external truth (true for everyone) and that it is accessible to pure reason. But taking a secular point of view, that has been shown to be suspect philosophically. Pure reason leads in different directions, depending on what assumptions you begin with. Postmodern people, who try to live without any assumptions, have become suspicious of the idea of universal truth. Hence, truth (and so doctrine) has gone out of fashion. It is relegated to the category of 'not important'. But Jesus said that the truth is important: 'You will know the truth and the truth will set you free' (John 8:32).

Actually, this 'doctrine doesn't matter, let's just be loving' approach is precisely the path taken by the old liberalism and theological modernism of the nineteenth and early twentieth centuries, but in a different disguise. They said, 'let's forget the doctrine because we don't believe it.' Today's evangelical Christians say they do believe it, but don't like the consequences of taking a definite stance with which other people might disagree. So instead they swing into the 'let's downplay the doctrine because it isn't important' mode. But thinking that doctrine is not important is halfway to not believing it.

However, Christian love without Christian truth is like a human body without bones – a jelly-like mess. God has made our bodies a beautiful balance of the hard and the soft, the bones and the flesh. And they need each other. The bones without the flesh is dead – a lifeless skeleton. But the flesh without the bones is obscene! So notice how love and truth go together for Paul. He writes: 'And this is my prayer: that your love may abound more and more in knowledge and depth of insight, so that you may be able to discern what is best...' (1:9-10).

Truth is what we know, and love should grow through knowledge of it. Holding to the truth with integrity is mature. This is grown-up Christianity.

MAKING PROGRESS ON THE JOURNEY?

With this in mind, there are some areas of church life which we can highlight and which we need to keep an eye on in order to be a church with gospel integrity.

Expository Preaching: If we are married to the truth of Christ then we must be married to the Bible. God's Word must be at the centre of church life. Pastors are to preach the Word, in season and out of season (2 Tim. 4:2). Let's hear no complaints about opening our Bibles every Sunday. In a mature church, people love to hear good Bible teaching. It is the spiritual food which feeds their faith. It is the light to their path through life. It is the inspiration and joy of their souls. It brings about the renewing of their minds and thinking. Jesus said: 'Man does not live on bread alone but on every word that comes from the mouth of God' (Matt. 4:4).

Systematic theology: But, having said that, there can be a commitment to expository preaching which is so nuanced by biblical theology that it misses the wood for the trees. Taking this line exclusively leads to only preaching that which is peculiar to a certain book of the Bible, the message of Micah or Colossians etc. But this can mean that something as foundational as say, the sovereignty of God, which is assumed by every book in the Bible, gets neglected or is never explained in detail. It rarely comes centre stage in its own right. In the name of expository preaching we can neglect systematic theology, and people fail to have an organised grasp of Christian doctrine and propositional truth. Christians may have heard all kinds of encouraging or challenging messages from this or that Bible book. It fed their souls for the upcoming week. It was inspirational. But they have been left with little overall grasp of what they believe.

What I am arguing is that, while not neglecting consecutive Bible exposition, there is also a need for topical preaching. What does the whole Bible say about God's sovereignty? What does the whole Bible say about the cross? What is the biblical overview on gender issues? Bible truth is not less than propositional truth. And that takes us to the fact that leaders should teach the doctrinal standards of their church. Sometimes, leaders need to teach the church's statement of faith from the Bible. It means a return to systematic theology, not just biblical theology.

Thinking: A return to systematic theology will help renew the minds of church members – getting them thinking in a biblical way. We enjoy stories and the Bible is a story. But God has also made us to be logical thinkers. A structured, cogent understanding of Christianity provides believers with a grid of truth by which to discern the way to live in a changing world. A reasonable faith, grounded in Scripture, will equip God's children in an all-round way to see through lies and to choose what is best. There are many exciting and different ways of encouraging such renewing of their minds. Here are two examples.

A friend of mine does a kind of seminar by walking a group of Christians around a shopping mall armed with the ten commandments. 'Now look at what is here,' he says, 'and assess what you see in terms of God's laws.' Then into a cafe for coffee and discussion. It helps people to think about life in terms, not of feel good (everything in the shopping mall is designed to make you feel good), but in terms of Christian truth.

Or, taking a different tack, I once heard Os Guinness, a great apologist for Christian faith, speak about raising his children. He used to play a game with them with TV adverts. They would be watching something, but during the advert break he would encourage them to keep watching and 'spot the lie' in the advert – there usually is one! It was to train them in thinking in a biblical way. Christian transformation takes place not by 'feely/ touchy' but by the renewing of our minds (Rom. 12:2).

Belonging: There is a New Testament doctrine of church membership. The church was made up of the local congregation who had committed themselves to Christ and to the apostles' doctrine. Those who were counted as part of the church believed what the apostles taught, and in the light of that commitment they promised to do their best to live in accordance with that truth as part of the church community. This is what baptism implied. We find this for example as the result of Pentecost in Acts 2. With the coming of the Spirit, Peter preached Christ to the crowds and those who accepted his message were baptised and added to the number of the church. Of these we read: 'They devoted themselves to the apostles' teaching and to the fellowship, to the breaking of bread and to prayer' (Acts 2:42). It was a church founded on truth. Starting with the truth of the gospel which the apostles declared, the church devoted themselves to understanding it and doing their best to live it out in practice together. This is integrity.

The membership of the Jerusalem church was not composed of perfect people. We all fail. But it was made up of those who believed the apostles' teaching, were seeking to live God's way, and were repentant over their sins – not seeking to defend them or justify them. That's why there was an ongoing focus on 'the breaking of bread' – the Lord's Supper where we confess our continuing need for forgiveness and celebrate the fact that Christ has paid for our sins. This is part and parcel of a lifestyle which is congruent with the gospel, which fits with the truth (Titus 2:1-2). Membership is a way of both guarding and celebrating the truth. By it the church says, 'This is what we believe, and we are all in this together!'

The mature church has a definite membership based on gospel integrity in belief and behaviour. This is maturity.

HOPE

What will help us to keep true to the gospel and living it out? What will spur us on to integrity and maturity? It is our hope for the future.

The apostle Paul points to the Christian's great and certain future as he closes this chapter in Philippians. There's a battle for truth and integrity to be engaged. There is a war with sin to be fought, which is ongoing and hard. He tells us that, since we do not really belong to this present world, we should not give in to it and its errors. We are citizens of heaven: 'And we eagerly await a Saviour from there, the Lord Jesus Christ,' who will transform everything (v. 20). There is ultimate victory for what is right. There is a new world waiting. This is the Christian's hope for the future, and as we set our minds and hearts on this coming reality it will help us to say 'No' to heresy and sin and to live out the gospel with integrity. Jesus Christ is coming again.

Christ's return brings our salvation to completion and is a primary source of strength and inspiration for Christians and for the churches. Martin Luther had a personal crest which helped him to keep in mind the Saviour from heaven and the heavenly salvation which He brings. The crest consists of a black cross on a red heart, inside a white rose, on a background of sky-blue surrounded by a circle of gold. In a letter of 1530 to Lazarus Spengler he explained the symbolism of his crest and how it summed up his theology. He wrote:

> There is first to be a cross, black and placed in a heart which should be of its natural colour, so that I myself would be reminded that faith in the Crucified saves us. For if one believes from the heart he will be justified. Even though it is a black cross which mortifies and which should also hurt us, yet it leaves the heart in its natural colour and does not ruin nature; that is, the cross does not kill but keeps man alive. For the just man lives by faith, but by faith in the Crucified One.
>
> Such a heart is to be in the midst of a white rose, to symbolise that faith gives joy, comfort and peace; in a word it places the believer into a white joyful rose; for this faith does not give peace and joy as the world gives and, therefore, the rose is to be white and not red, for white is the colour of the spirits and all the angels. Such a rose is to be in a sky-blue field, symbolising that such joy in the Spirit and faith is a beginning of the future heavenly joy; it is already a part of faith, and is grasped through hope, even though not yet manifest. And around this field is a golden ring, symbolising that in heaven such blessedness lasts forever and has no end, and in addition is precious beyond all joy and goods, just as gold is the most valuable and precious metal.[5]

It is in contemplating the riches of this great salvation, known fully at Christ's return, that God's people find strength to 'stand firm' (4:1).

An encouragement to maturity would be that we find that heaven and the Second Coming are preached more often from our pulpits.

---

5   *Luther's Works,* volume 49 (Fortress Press, 1957), pp. 358-9.

Chapter 5

The Mature Church's **Stability**

This may not be so true of other countries, but the United Kingdom seems to have suffered a general dumbing down of culture in the last few decades.

I was reminded of this recently when a student from our own church spent a year at a German university as part of his course. He is a thoughtful, hardworking lad, but even for him the change came like a cold shower. Of his German experience he said to his parents, 'University here is for grown ups!' In other words, it is taken very seriously.

At his German university, people don't live on campus. They go there to work from 9 until 5. They are expected to work hard. There are not lots of different cafes and bars on campus to hang out in. There's just one government subsidised canteen. They get on with study like a job, and the job is to learn the subject which will make them competent in their chosen field. The students are there first and foremost to work.

When you compare this with the way different universities advertise themselves and compete for students in this country, we see the difference is very marked. Often, when universities in the UK seek to tempt students to apply to them, the pitch is put in terms of the social opportunities, friendships, the drinking and nightlife to be had in their town or city. It is a completely different philosophy that is really quite juvenile. It may be a generalisation, but in Germany going to university appears a serious undertaking, whereas here it is pictured as more about having a laugh, a good time (and picking up a degree on the way).

IS 'FUN' THE WAY FORWARD?

I know this is only one example, but that same spirit of dumbing down has transferred itself to many areas of life, including churches in this country. The gospel can easily become just another way of fulfilling adolescent needs.

This has deep roots. In his book *The Juvenilization of American Christianity*,[1] chronicling the changes in the US church during the mid-twentieth century, Thomas Bergler has a telling chapter entitled, 'How to have fun, be popular and save the world at the same time.' Fun? Popularity? They are indeed particular priorities for teenagers. But that's not how the mission to save the world worked out for the early church. Yes, there was joy. Paul tells us to 'rejoice in the Lord always'. But this joy was often in the context of opposition, trouble and even persecution. We have to step back a little and grow up. We have to get serious.

In Philippians 4:2-13 Paul deals with various challenges both he and the church at Philippi are facing. The Christian life is not always a walk in the park. We can't always have fun. We can't always be popular. His concern is not about the church having a good time but how it can remain constant and content amid difficulties. He wants to see spiritual stability.

> *I plead with Euodia and I plead with Syntyche to be of the same mind in the Lord. Yes, and I ask you, my true companion, help these women*

---

1   *The Juvenilization of American Christianity*, p. 147.

*since they have contended at my side in the cause of the gospel, along
with Clement and the rest of my co-workers, whose names are in the
book of life.*

*Rejoice in the Lord always. I will say it again: Rejoice! Let your
gentleness be evident to all. The Lord is near. Do not be anxious
about anything, but in every situation, by prayer and petition, with
thanksgiving, present your requests to God. And the peace of God, which
transcends all understanding, will guard your hearts and your minds
in Christ Jesus.*

*Finally, brothers and sisters, whatever is true, whatever is noble,
whatever is right, whatever is pure, whatever is lovely, whatever is
admirable—if anything is excellent or praiseworthy—think about
such things. Whatever you have learned or received or heard from me, or
seen in me—put it into practice. And the God of peace will be with you.*

*I rejoiced greatly in the Lord that at last you renewed your concern
for me. Indeed, you were concerned, but you had no opportunity to show
it. I am not saying this because I am in need, for I have learned to be
content whatever the circumstances. I know what it is to be in need,
and I know what it is to have plenty. I have learned the secret of being
content in any and every situation, whether well fed or hungry, whether
living in plenty or in want. I can do all this through him who gives
me strength.*

This is a section which mentions troubles that Christians face.
In the New Testament we find Christians having to face a great
variety of challenges to their faith. How are we going to remain
firm as we face ordinary troubles like poverty or serious illness?
How are we going to stand strong when a well-known Christian
leader falls into public disgrace? How shall we cope if we fall foul
of the government authorities because of what we stand for?

Not panicking or being overwhelmed by discouragement
amid various difficulties is a mark of grown-up Christianity.
Stability amid the storm is a sign of a well-seasoned and robust

faith. And such a reliable and staunch church becomes an anchor for others – a source of comfort and security.

How to remain sound and reliable under pressure is a pressing question for us. Why? It is because, apart from the regular challenges of the Christian life, all the signs point to the growing possibility of Bible-believing churches in this country running into some degree of persecution. The more we are faithful to the gospel, the more we stand out from the world, is bringing increasing opposition from our 'feel-good' Western society.

REMAINING SOUND AND RELIABLE

Bible churches are no strangers to a variety of troubles. In Philippians 4, we find problems of two different kinds. They come from inside and outside.

BROKEN RELATIONSHIPS WITHIN THE CHURCH

Two women in the church in Philippi had fallen out with each other. 'I plead with Euodia and I plead with Syntyche to be of the same mind in the Lord' (v. 2). These women were Christians, whose names were written in the book of life (v. 3). Furthermore they had worked hard for the gospel alongside Paul (v. 3). They were the kind of women others in the church would look up to and see as role models. Perhaps they were elders' wives? Perhaps one of them, or both, were dedicated single women who worked hard for Christ? When prominent people in a congregation are at loggerheads it destabilises the church. It is so discouraging. How do we cope?

The situation can become a major hindrance to progress as whatever plans or ideas are floated in a church, if one is for them the other is bound to be vociferously against them. Unity is eroded. Fellowship is damaged. There is an atmosphere in the church you can cut with a knife. It is so serious that Paul 'pleads' for unity and wants the 'loyal yoke-fellow' – probably the pastor at Philippi – to try to bring about reconciliation (v. 3). Such troubles can wreck a church.

This is not the only way to take verses 4-9, but it is possible that these verses are particularly relevant to broken relationships within a church. They may even be Paul's advice as to what the pastor should be talking to Euodia and Syntyche about as he seeks to restore their friendship. Think about it:

Rejoicing: 'Rejoice in the Lord always. I will say it again. Rejoice!' (v. 4). When we take our eyes off the Lord and His goodness to us in the gospel, we can become jaundiced in our outlook and attitudes and be prone to pick holes in other people.

Gentleness: 'Let your gentleness be evident to all. The Lord is near' (v. 5). When we forget that the Lord is watching and that, one day, we will give an account to Him we might feel at liberty to treat others harshly. We need to treat others in a way which pleases the Christ who has forgiven us and treated us far better than we deserve.

Peace: 'Do not be anxious about anything, but in everything...present your requests to God. And the peace of God...will guard your hearts...' (vv. 6-7). When we cease to bring our worries to the Lord in prayer and trust Him concerning them, we can start comparing our lot with that of others and become jealous and say unkind things. This is a source of friction. But when we know God's transcendent peace, we don't feel the need to contend with others.

Thinking: '...whatever is true, whatever is noble...think on these things' (v. 8). If we train our minds to reflect on what is noble, right and good it well help us see the best in other people. It will lead us to be thankful for them instead of critical of them.

Behaviour: 'Whatever you have learned or received or heard from me, or seen in me – put it into practice. And the God of peace will be with you' (v. 9). If we can find a good role-model like the apostle Paul to pattern ourselves on, then when faced with provocation, we will find ourselves asking, 'What would Paul do in this situation?' And that will help us to respond more graciously rather than giving some unhelpful knee-jerk reaction.

These can be seen as some practical suggestions about how to restore and maintain peace between people in the church. Such a church will be more likely to look after each other and stand strong. It will be a church with stability.

ONGOING OPPOSITION FROM THE OUTSIDE WORLD

Paul's life had not turned out to be one of fun and popularity. As he writes, he is in prison and in need because he is suffering persecution for the sake of the gospel (vv. 10-13). There is also the hint in verse 15 of being let down by other Christians, who unlike the Philippians gave no support to Paul in the midst of his trials.

As I have already indicated, we live at a time when our churches are having to swim against the tide in the Western world. We believe in God in a society that doesn't. We take our ideas from the Bible when that is the last place the majority of our fellow citizens would look for help. We preach Christ as the only way of salvation in a country that has come to insist there are many ways to find God. We stand for male–female marriage at a time when marriage has been redefined. We are pro-life in a land that is militantly pro-choice. We believe in male servant-headship in both family and the church, because that is what the Bible teaches, at a time when gender is said to be fluid and all authority oppressive. We believe that parents have the right and the responsibility to care and decide on their children's education, when governments are arrogating that right for themselves. And we could add to that list. In so many ways then, the church is countercultural. We are on a collision course with the powers that be. So how are we going to cope with being unpopular and with what appears to be the inevitable increasing conflict of interests?

What Paul writes about how he learned to cope with prison and the other ups and downs of life should be of particular interest to us. Whatever his circumstances, whether in need or not, he has learned how to stay strong, satisfied and steady. 'I have learned to be content whatever the circumstances. I know what it is to be in need, and I know what it is to have plenty. I have learned the secret of being content in any and every situation, whether well fed or hungry, whether living in plenty or in want. I can do all this through him who gives me strength' (vv. 11-13).

Notice it is the Lord Himself who is the key to finding contentment and strength whatever our circumstances. 'I can do all things through him...' This might sound a little pious and super-spiritual, but it is not. We do believe in a living Lord, who is personally present with us through His Holy Spirit, and who cares about us and provides us with strength. We believe He sees us and hears us. He is able to 'strengthen you with power through his Spirit in your inner being' (Eph. 3:16).

Here's an example: John Lennox, until recently a professor of mathematics at Oxford University, used to travel behind the Iron Curtain in the days of Communism. He writes of meeting a man who had been detained in a Siberian labour camp for the crime of teaching children from the Bible. 'He described to me (says Lennox) how he had seen things no man should see. I listened, thinking how little I really knew about life, and wondering how I would have fared under his circumstances. As if he read my thoughts he suddenly said: "You couldn't cope with that, could you?" Embarrassed, I stumbled out something like: "No, I'm sure you are right." He grinned and said: "Nor could I! I was a man who fainted at the sight of his own blood, let alone that of others. But what I discovered in the labour camp was this: God does not help us face theoretical situations but real ones. Like you, I couldn't imagine how one could cope in the Gulag. But once there I found that God met me, exactly as Jesus promised His disciples when He was preparing them for victimisation and persecution."[2]

It is in the Lord that we find our stability, even in the most trying of situations.

A PATH TO AVOID

Paul can do everything through Christ. However, the temptation in our touchy-feely therapy culture is to replace the Lord by the church; to substitute people for God. We can begin to look for strength and comfort primarily from our friends in the fellowship rather than from Christ Himself.

Of course, we can enjoy the help and care the church can give us. There is nothing wrong with that – except when it begins to push our relationship with Christ Himself to one side. That's when things go wrong. Replacing looking to God with looking to people happens in a number of ways.

We are so sensitised to emotions and hurts that we cannot bear to see anyone in pain and we rush round feeling that we must fix everything for them. We want to make them feel good and we can usually make them feel better by giving them lots of love and attention. But when we do that, there can be a temptation for them to become dependent on us rather than on the Lord. This doesn't have to happen, but it can; and when it does it is very unhelpful.

Further, we in the church who are looking after such people can begin to feel we are important, in a way that is less than

---

2   John Lennox, *Against the Flow: The Inspiration of Daniel in an Age of Relativism* (Monarch, 2017), pp. 150-1.

helpful, and to like that importance. A little pride sneaks in. We can come to imagine that we are somehow irreplaceable. Simultaneously our needy friends like us caring and we enjoy their expressions of thanks. And so we become co-dependent. Carers can start living on the appreciation they receive rather than on the Lord. It is a retrograde step.

What we need to bear in mind in such situations is this. Yes, we should look after the needy in the church, but realise that the things which we can do for them are ultimately limited. It is only the Lord who can touch their hearts and truly heal their wounds. Only the Spirit can transform things on the inside. Understanding this will keep a right balance. It will drive us to prayer. Only the Lord can fix them. Their problems are far deeper than their emotions. They need the Lord, not us ultimately. They need the change He brings.

But easier than change is attention and so, if we are not careful, we make them into attention junkies. And then it can get worse. Because 'victims' are still sinners they can become manipulators too. And soon the 'you weren't there for me!' syndrome starts. Dear church members are running themselves ragged and feeling guilty because they can't fix someone's problems and be on twenty-four-hour call. Hear me. The church can't fix anybody's problems. Only the Lord can.

We have got ourselves into this by buying into this immature, emotion-centred culture instead of having the biblical realism to always point people to Christ. Churches and individual Christians need to care, but they also need to be mature enough to discern when they can do no more. We need to be mature enough to say 'No' sometimes and mature enough to take the flak that might come. This, in a sense, puts a limit on, or gives wisdom to, what we have seen from Philippians 2. Yes, we should serve as Christ served. But the church is only the help, it is not the solution. The mature church is a servant, but it knows it is not God; it is not the Lord.

THE PATH TO PROGRESS

Instead, the model to follow is found in Gethsemane. Here is Jesus facing enormous trouble. 'My soul is overwhelmed to the point of death,' He tells His disciples in Matthew 26:38. His friends are around Him for support. The church should indeed do what it can to support. But notice where is Jesus looking for the strength He really needs? Not to the twelve. Not to Peter, James or John. What a 'let down' that would have been! They fell asleep. His source of strength is found in heaven. He is on His knees looking to God.

We must do the same as we face troubles and we must help others who are hurting by pointing them in the same direction. Paul says in 4:13: 'I can do everything through him who gives me strength.' In practical terms, this means we must get the church, and the individuals who make up the church, back to the old disciplines of personal prayer and Bible study, those means of grace by which we foster a personal relationship with the Lord. When our friends are facing troubles we must get together and pray to God for them. We must help them to seek the Lord and to walk with God in their troubles. This is the way to spiritual maturity.

Let me tell you, if the trouble of persecution ever does break out again in our land, it is ultimately only the strength which comes from a deep and personal relationship with the Lord that will sustain us. This is what we need to nurture constantly.

ONE DIRECTION

In order to hammer home the point, let's go back over the passage we have focused on in this chapter. As we run through this catalogue of various kinds of troubles, we find Paul consistently pointing in one direction. What is his teaching about how to cope, how to deal with difficulty? The answer is our personal relationship with the Lord.

You two women, stop fighting because you are 'in the Lord', and the Lord and His work are far more important than whatever it is you fell out about! So agree with each other 'in the Lord' (v. 2).

Instead of being overcome by anxiety (v. 6), you are to rejoice 'in the Lord' and bring your problems to the Lord in prayer and be at peace, leaving them with Him.

When it comes to finding contentment amid privation and difficulty, Paul points to Christ (v. 13). He is the one in whom we will find strength. He is the one through whom we can do all things.

So, you see that amid all the varied trials and difficulties which Paul lists here, his ultimate focus is on the Lord. It is trust in Him that will bring the Philippians contentedness and stability. He too must be our source of strength and stability.

Chapter 6

The Mature Church's **Generosity**

Money is always going to be a big issue for a 'feel good' society. We have our five senses: sight, hearing, taste, smell and touch. Money allows you to see what you like, hear what you like, taste what you like, smell as good as you like, and touch what you like. Money is power for pleasure.

The great pleasure idols of our times are the seven 'f's: fitness, fashion, food, football, families, fornication and foreign holidays. Money opens the door to all of these and more, all of which can be misused. Perhaps that is why the apostle Paul describes the love of money as 'a root of all kinds of evil' (1 Tim. 6:10).

Money empowers our idols, and idols, of whatever sort, deaden our spiritual sensitivity. We change into what we worship.[1] Having described how insensitive and incapable idols are, the psalmist tells us that those who make idols become like them (Ps. 115:3-8). They are like the White Witch in Narnia who had the power to turn living creatures to stone. They are like an anaesthetic which numbs us to spiritual reality. They

---

1   Greg Beale's book, *We Become What We Worship* (Apollos, IVP, 2008), gives a full explanation of this phenomenon.

bring a dementia, a forgetfulness of the things of God. They bring spiritual deadness.

That's how Christians and churches lose their spiritual edge. The salt loses its taste. We can become good for nothing Christians and fit for nothing churches (Luke 14:34-35). Money can conduct us down that road. Activating our idols can lead us away from maturity and into shallowness.

But, of course, it is not money itself that is bad. It all depends on how we use it. When God gives us money, He blesses us, but He expects us to be generous with what He has given. To be generous with our finances is the grown-up Christian's attitude. It shows that we control our money without it controlling us. It shows that we are serving God, not Mammon. It shows we obey one Master (Matt. 6:24).

The Philippian church showed this maturity in generosity. While Paul was in prison, they had sent Epaphroditus, probably one of the church's leaders, to 'take care of my needs,' says Paul (2:25). He had brought a generous gift from the church. As Paul draws his letter to a close, he expresses his thanks for the generosity of the Philippians. Here is what he says in 4:14-20:

> Yet it was good of you to share in my troubles. Moreover, as you Philippians know, in the early days of your acquaintance with the gospel, when I set out from Macedonia, not one church shared with me in the matter of giving and receiving, except you only; for even when I was in Thessalonica, you sent me aid more than once when I was in need. Not that I desire your gifts; what I desire is that more be credited to your account. I have received full payment and have more than enough. I am amply supplied, now that I have received from Epaphroditus the gifts you sent. They are a fragrant offering, an acceptable sacrifice, pleasing to God. And my God will meet all your needs according to the riches of his glory in Christ Jesus.
>
> To our God and Father be glory for ever and ever. Amen.

The Philippian church was a church of givers. When, at the beginning of the letter, Paul referred to their partnership in the gospel (1:5), and their sharing in God's grace with him (1:7), it was their support of him and their financial contribution to the gracious cause of the gospel which was in his mind.

We can see something of this in the narrative of Acts. Philippi was a major city in the province of Macedonia. After Paul left there, he had suffered a torrid time in Thessalonica, having to flee for his life after just a three-week mission (Acts 17:9). From there he had travelled to Berea, then on to Athens, then Corinth. While in Corinth he was forced to take up his trade of tentmaking to support himself (Acts 18:1-3). But then we read, 'When Silas and Timothy came from Macedonia, Paul devoted himself exclusively to preaching...' (Acts 18:5). It seems that they brought gifts which meant that Paul did not have to worry about having to earn a wage and so could give himself wholly to his ministry. Our verses here in Philippians 4, particularly verses 15 and 16, indicate that the gift came from Philippi. No other churches were involved.

SACRIFICIAL GENEROSITY

We can fill out what we know about the giving of the Philippians from elsewhere in the New Testament. Paul's ministry included a desire for the Gentile churches to send support to the Jewish churches back in Palestine. They faced a period of suffering connected with the famine which the prophet Agabus had indicated would happen (Acts 11:27-30).

Paul's collections for this cause were ongoing. Not only did he want to use giving to build unity across the churches with different ethnic backgrounds, but he also saw that such giving would be a step towards Christian maturity and bring a blessing to those who gave.

He mentions these collections as he writes his second letter to the church in Corinth: 'And now, brothers, we want you to know about the grace God has given the Macedonian churches. Out of the most extreme trial, their overflowing joy and extreme poverty welled up in rich generosity. For I testify that they gave as much as they were able, and even beyond their ability. Entirely on their own, they urgently pleaded with us for the privilege of sharing in this service to the saints' (2 Cor. 8:1-4).

Among those Macedonian churches would have been the church at Philippi. What stands out is the sacrificial nature of their giving. They didn't just give when they could afford it. They gave when they couldn't afford it. It hurt them to give. But nevertheless they gave. This shows something of the intensity of the love they had for Paul (and other Christians) reflected in the opening verses of the epistle.

To put it bluntly, the Philippians gave in a way that kept them poor. These days Christians and churches like that are few and far between.

PAUL'S TAKE ON GIVING

As he says 'thank you' to the Philippian church for the gift they had sent him through Epaphroditus, Paul teaches us many things about Christian giving. It is good to give to the poor, as we have noted, but what is specifically in view in these verses is giving to support Christian ministry. Here are seven brief things to note.

Giving is beautiful. Paul says of their gift, 'it was good of you' (v. 14). The word 'good' is related to the idea of beauty or being splendidly appropriate. It is morally gorgeous. It is reminiscent of Jesus' words about the woman who had anointed Him with expensive perfume. 'Why are you bothering her? She has done a beautiful thing to me' (Mark 14:6).

Giving is service. They shared in Paul's troubles (v. 14). They shared in the matter of giving and receiving (v. 15). To share is to serve. Where you share you help. You help bear the load. You help with the cost. You may not be able to go to the mission field yourself, or have a gift in evangelism, but as you give, you have a part in the work. You do your share. You pull your weight.

Giving is rare. Giving like that of the Philippians is not as common as it ought to be. Paul records that for a certain period 'not one church shared with me in the matter of giving and receiving, but you only' (v. 15). And the point becomes clearer in the next verse: 'for even when I was in Thessalonica, you sent me aid again and again' (v. 16). Most people are up for a one-off gift. But the Philippians were repeated and constant givers.

Giving is creditable. This is highlighted as Paul explains his joy at receiving what they had sent. He says, 'Not that I am looking for a gift, but I am looking for what may be credited to your account' (v. 17). God takes notice when we give and is pleased. Jesus took notice of the poor widow's sacrificial few pence (Luke 21:1-4). He commended her to His disciples, saying that she had given to God more than all the rich.

Giving is payment. Paul had done a great gospel work in Philippi. Though he never charged for preaching the gospel, yet it is good when Christians realise that they owe something to those who minister to them, especially to those through whom they were saved. Paul says, 'I have received full payment and even more' (v. 18). In this sense, giving to Christian work is not an option, it is a duty (1 Tim. 5:17-18).

Giving is worship. The gifts which Epaphroditus brought from Philippi are described as 'a fragrant offering, an acceptable sacrifice, pleasing to God' (v. 18). To worship is to humble ourselves and to give glory to God, thankfully acknowledging His rightful supremacy over us. Giving is a very practical way to do this. By supporting Christian workers we are signifying the priority of God and of Christ's gospel in our lives.

Giving is wise. Giving is a smart thing to do because God looks after those who look after His cause. We do this as we support Christian workers. Reflecting on their gift brought to him in prison, Paul promises: 'And my God will meet all your needs according to his glorious riches in Christ Jesus' (v. 19). He doesn't promise them luxuries, but he does promise that their necessities would be met. Jesus taught us concerning food and drink and clothing: 'But seek first his kingdom and his righteousness, and all these things will be given to you as well' (Matt. 6:33).

THE DEAD SEA

When a church doesn't give as it should, it becomes moribund. The flow of God's blessing gets clogged up as the church looks after only itself. This is not how it should be. It loses life.

Here is a striking picture to bear in mind. Running along the eastern border of Israel is the wonderful River Jordan. It is a source of life, refreshment and fruitfulness. But it ends in the Dead Sea, the lowest point on land on the earth's surface.

Why is the Dead Sea dead? Because although the Jordan river is its primary inflow, it has no outflows. The water runs into this great lake, but there it stays until it simply evaporates under the heat of the Middle Eastern sun. Because the water has no way out, the lifegiving H2O is continually burned off, leaving only the minerals it carries. The Dead Sea is left with high concentrations of salt in which nothing can live. Its salinity is something like 34 per cent. This makes the Dead Sea very easy to swim in or float around in. You can even sit in it, buoyed up by the high-density saline solution, and read a newspaper without getting it wet. But instead of being a place of life, there is death.

When churches fail to give, they like the Dead Sea lose spiritual life. God's blessing flows in, but they keep it all for themselves. There is no substantial outflow. They build a bigger sanctuary. They pay large salaries to their staff. They make things very comfortable. 'Business' appears to be booming. But it is a church that is declining spiritually. It is taking a very different path from the way of the Saviour who calls us to deny ourselves, take up our cross and follow Him (Mark 8:34). The church may produce 'Christians' of a sort, but whether the Lord would recognise them as such may be debatable.

The words of Jesus to us all are, 'Freely you have received, freely give' (Matt. 10:8). This is the way which brings life to others and life to us.

PROGRESS IN GENEROSITY

When we give, we are making a practical statement that our true resource is not how much we have in the bank, but God and His grace. That is the direction of maturity as Christians and as churches. Here are a few challenges to consider.

YOUNGER PEOPLE

Research indicates that today's younger people – millennials – are good at giving to causes which touch them emotionally. There is nothing wrong with that. It is good to be moved to give. But the research shows they are not so good at giving to non-emotional causes. They will give when they see TV footage of starving children in Africa – as we all should – because it makes them well up and feel they have to do something. But they are not good at giving regularly to sustain a work which may be essential but doesn't torture their heartstrings. They are also better at giving to one-off needs than being committed to giving regularly and substantially. We have to step back a moment. If this is true, we need to realise that such a pattern of giving is not going to provide long term for a pastor and his family, or maintain an evangelist's ministry, or keep a missionary on the field. These things are just too everyday. This is very serious for the long-term future of the church and the gospel.

OLDER PEOPLE

How can older people think about giving?

It is not only younger people who require challenging. Middle-aged and older folk need to look at themselves. The so-called 'baby-boomers' are the post-war generation born between 1946 and 1964. They are now in their mid-50s through to mid-70s, and they make up 21.3 per cent of the UK population. These people are now, generally speaking, the people with money. A statement from the National Office of Statistics in April 2018 made me sit up. 'The net household property wealth of those aged between 60 and 62 is 17 times greater than those aged between 30 and 32.'[2] Seventeen times more wealth! That is a lot. Therefore it seems that older Christians are those with the greatest responsibility for the finances of Christ's kingdom before God. We cannot say, 'I'm retired. It's now time for me to simply enjoy myself and spend what belongs to me on myself.' Jesus taught, 'From everyone who has been given much, much will be demanded; and from the one who has been entrusted with much, much more will be asked' (Luke 12:48). How can older people think about giving? While 'baby-boomers' have their health, they need to make every effort to give as much as possible to the work of the Lord. As they move towards their

---

2   No doubt our wealth will have been drastically affected by the economic consequences of the coronavirus epidemic. But that is likely to have affected all age groups in the same proportion – so the basic point still stands.

later years, there are obviously a number of other considerations which come into play. They may have to think about paying for a care home at some point. Perhaps most of the finance is tied up in their property if they own a house. You can't easily give that capital away until death takes you. Those who are parents will have a concern to leave some kind of legacy to their children. That is understandable. But with such a lot of money compared to younger people, older Christians should be careful not to lose sight of the needs of churches and mission. Maybe it is wise to seek financial advice, but to do so with a clear intention of leaving as much as possible to Christian work.

TITHING

We need to be aware of the power of the acquisitive spirit. The 'feel good' society encourages us, after paying our bills, to spend our money on ourselves. 'There's just this life,' secular people say, 'live it to the full,' by which they mean spare no expense to have fun. When such thoughts, even unconsciously, take hold of Christians, giving descends to the minimum. There is so much to spend our money on. The consumer society sets before us a vast marketplace. We want the best for ourselves. We feel we must have the best for our kids. The idea of tithing our money and giving a tenth to God's work is increasingly out of fashion in the churches. Some research shows that in the United States those who tithe now make up only between 10 per cent and 25 per cent of congregations. We make some theological point about tithing being Old Testament and use that as an excuse for ourselves. But the resulting level of giving, once we abandon tithing, becomes less and hardly any sacrifice at all. This is very far from grown-up discipleship. The New Testament describes the life of a true Christian as one of 'living sacrifice' (Rom. 12:1).

Instead of a grudging attitude towards money, today's church must cultivate a new generosity. It is a great thing to give. And giving will do great things for us and for the churches. "'Bring the full tithe into the storehouse.... Test me in this,' says the Lord Almighty, 'and see if I will not throw open the floodgates of heaven and pour out so much blessing that you will not have room for it'" (Mal. 3:10).

Conclusion and Coronavirus:

Why Did God Shut the Churches?

As we come to the end of this book, I have a question. It is this. Why did God shut the churches?

I am referring, of course, to what happened in early 2020. A deadly virus spread across the world and governments had to respond to this enormous threat. I mentioned this pandemic in the introduction. Rightly the churches decided to close their doors in order to respect social distancing and to help kerb the spread of the epidemic. We can't love God at the expense of endangering our neighbours' lives.

Scripture is clear that God is sovereign and tragedies such as the spread of coronavirus are not beyond His control but are under His control. He sends the calamities as well as the good things we receive every day (Lam. 3:38; Isa. 45:7). So, ultimately, it was God who shut the churches. This is something unprecedented in history.

God's purpose

God is not senseless. Therefore, we must conclude that this virus, which has caused so much grief, came with a purpose. I cannot pretend to fully understand the ways of God. The Lord addresses us and says, 'As the heavens are higher than the earth, so are my ways higher than your ways and my thoughts than your thoughts' (Isa. 55:9). But we do know that whatever God's providence sends on the earth will, in the long run, be for the good of His people and His church.

John Flavel, the Puritan pastor of Dartmouth in Devon, wrote this: 'If the means and instruments employed to bestow mercy to the people of God are seriously considered, who can but confess that there are tools of all sorts and sizes in the workshop of providence and a most skilful hand uses them.'[1]

The skilful hand of God closed church buildings across the world. Yes, Christians carried on in their faith and maintained fellowship and worship as best they could. In that sense the churches were not closed. But what was the Lord saying to His churches in doing this? It may well be that He was saying different things to different churches in different parts of the world. But as we look at what happened, unique in church history, we cannot but conclude that not only the world, but the church has been sobered. It is as if we have all been brought down to earth. We have been reminded of life and death, of heaven and hell. We have been brought back to basics as to what the gospel and therefore what the church is really about.

TIME TO GROW UP

Was the Lord telling many churches in the West that they had got too distracted with juvenile things? I think perhaps He was. Our minds had become taken up with making church fun, how we look, what image we projected. Our preachers had become too concerned to tick their own boxes concerning 'sharp' sermons than with speaking of Christ from the heart to the hearts of

---

1   *The Mystery of Providence*, John Flavel, quoted in *Voices From the Past*,
     volume 1, p. 156.

their people. Our people had begun to idolise certain celebrity preachers, which is a stark, staring mark of immaturity (1 Cor. 3:1-4). Our desire for 'success' in terms of numbers meant many churches were letting go of meaningful church membership and the godly discipline which is the real mark of discipleship. With its glossy conferences, podcasts and music, Church had become almost a multi-million-dollar entertainment industry in the eyes of many. In a number of ways, through the gravity of the pandemic, I think the Lord was saying that we have to grow up.

If I'm right, even partially about the purpose of this plague which has swept the earth and closed the churches, then the need to leave childish ways behind is urgent and serious. God does not afflict His people at a whim. He does not bring such trouble upon us lightly. Therefore, we ought to think very carefully about this unprecedented and severe providence. As churches and individuals we need to humble ourselves and seek God as perhaps we have never done previously in our lifetimes.

It is the mark of a fool that he takes no heed of discipline (Prov. 15:5). It is the mocker who resents correction (Prov. 15:12). 'A rebuke impresses a man of discernment more than a hundred lashes a fool' (Prov. 17:10). Our God is a loving Father. He means the discipline of such a painful providence for our good. But we need to respond by seeking Him, and by seeking to obey Him. If we believe in a sovereign God who orders the course of our life and times, we cannot simply shrug our shoulders and carry on as before. We should at least stop and reflect.

GROWN UP FOR CHRIST

The purpose of this book is to point the way to growing up to maturity as Christians and as churches. So, in the light of where we have come to as churches in the twenty-first century, let's briefly put together the whole picture of what we have learned from Philippians.

We live in a secular society, which has become dominated by all kinds of ideas and influences which militate against our growing up in Christ. But we have been given a shock. The coronavirus has humbled everyone, including the church. Church for grown-ups? Post-lockdown we need to have a clear vision as to what we are aiming to be in order to live for Christ.

CHAPTER 1: QUALITY

A church should be composed of followers of Jesus who have a deep affection for one another in Christ, an affection which shows itself in practice. *The church should be lovingly mature.* The quality which Jesus looks for in a church is mature Christian love – love for others which is rooted in love for Jesus because of God's love for us. Notice this is a matter of the heart. It is not fundamentally an outward quality but an inward one. It shows itself in practical care, but its driving force is within. Different places have their own 'feel'. A factory or an office can have the 'feel' of efficiency. A supermarket can have the 'feel', the atmosphere of cleanliness and orderliness. But when you enter a church and come among God's people the quality you should be most aware of is one of love. Look at yourself. Look at your church. Is it there? And if it is there, thank God for it, but like Paul pray that it might grow 'more and more'.

CHAPTER 2: PRIORITY

A church should be made up of people whose top priority is spreading the gospel and building the kingdom. *The church needs to be missionally mature.* Notice I have used the phrase 'building the kingdom' not 'the church'. I have done that because in our superficiality 'building the church' has often been reduced to 'building our church'. Immature Christians see no further than their own congregation. Mature concern for evangelism is motivated by two things. These are (1) a desire for the glory of the name of the Lord Jesus Christ and (2) a desire to see poor hell-bound sinners saved from eternal destruction. Whether or not those people join our church comes much further down our 'bucket-list' of 'must haves'. Look at yourself. Look at your church. What is the real priority? The Bible would interpret such calamities as the coronavirus pandemic as a warning, a trumpet call wake-up to the world of the coming day of judgment. Do we long to see people saved?

CHAPTER 3: COMMUNITY

A church should be a gospel family serving one another in the humility of Christ. *We need to be collectively mature.* We live in a consumer culture where everything comes down to getting what you want and where people tend to be treated as 'customers' for whom the business provides a service. We have argued that church needs to be a place of service, but not service in the sense which we find in shops and supermarkets. Church should be about sacrificial service. No one should have to pay to be served in church. And church is not about the 'management' providing a service, but about everyone providing service to everyone else. Churches where the leadership treat church members as customers or 'punters' rather than brothers and sisters are missing the mark completely. A church is a community where people 'in humility consider others as better' than themselves.

CHAPTER 4: INTEGRITY

A church should be clear and unashamed as to what it believes and to positively live out in practice what it stands for on paper. *We need to be theologically mature.* In a time when emotion and the 'feel good' factor has dominated churches, there needs to be a return to clear thinking and practice. Many churches have become unbalanced and almost anti-intellectual in a way which threatens to depart from the gospel. We need to be clear about the primary truths of the gospel. Without in any way being abusive or unloving to people, the church has to draw lines in the sand about what it believes and what it does not believe, what behaviour is acceptable and what is not. We must be people and churches who take seriously that we are not of this world, but whose 'citizenship is in heaven' – that holy place.

CHAPTER 5: STABILITY

A church needs to have a resilience and steadiness in times of trouble that comes not just from a team spirit among each other but also from the Lord Himself. *We need to be spiritually mature.* The world is changing fast. Often it seems a very unstable place in which many people feel very insecure and even frightened about what might happen next. A grown-up church will be a place of refuge. It will be a loving haven in the storm. The people of the church will not always have a smooth life or have everything together. But they really do know a 'peace that passes understanding' and a contentment whatever their circumstances. That peace of God will come through prayer and true reliance on Christ. Grown-up Christians can say with the apostle Paul, 'I can do everything through him who gives me strength.'

CHAPTER 6: GENEROSITY

A church needs to love to give money away, especially to the support of those who serve Christ in the gospel. *We need to be financially mature* – which means breaking out of the 'money is everything' attitude of the world. The mature church takes seriously that it is impossible to serve two masters, God and money. But it loves to use its money to serve the cause of Christ and by giving to the poor and needy to store up treasure in heaven. A mature church has a deep appreciation for the generosity of God in the gospel and wants to emulate that generosity whenever it possibly can, knowing that God will meet all their needs 'according to his glorious riches in Christ Jesus'.

***

Taken seriously there is nothing middle of the road or boring about this maturity. It is radical. Jesus gave His all. He went to death – even the death of a cross – for us. Now here's the question. Will you give your all? Is that honestly your intention? Will you do whatever it takes to be and to build a mature church for Jesus? A church of grown-ups!

I believe that by the remarkable fact of God shutting the churches through the coronavirus, He is calling us to leave behind childish things and grow up.

JOHN BENTON

Resilient

How 2 Timothy
Teaches us to Bounce Back
in Christian Leadership

RESILIENT

HOW 2 TIMOTHY TEACHES US TO BOUNCE BACK IN CHRISTIAN LEADERSHIP

JOHN BENTON

Being a Christian leader is a huge privilege. It is also a huge challenge. Paul, a man who knew how tough it could be, wrote a letter to his young friend who was at a crossroads in the ministry, to encourage resilience in the spiritual battle. John Benton looks at what 2 Timothy has to say about finding strength, recovering from discouragement and keeping going as a Christian leader.

This book is a wonderful example of how God's word speaks afresh in every generation. With a careful exegetical eye and a kind pastor's heart, Dr Benton unpacks 2 Timothy showing us the true roots of and great need for resilience in pastoral ministry. This is an excellent resource for pastors to keep on keeping on.

Robin Weekes
Minister, Emmanuel Church, Wimbledon, London

ISBN 978-1-5271-0210-1

BRIAN CROFT &
JAMES B. CARROLL
FOREWORD BY MARK CLIFTON

FACING
SNARLS&
SCOWLS

PREACHING THROUGH
HOSTILITY, APATHY, AND ADVERSITY
IN CHURCH REVITALIZATION

Facing Snarls and Scowls

Preaching through Hostility, Apathy and Adversity in Church Revitalization

Brian Croft and James B. Carroll

Pastor, the hard work of church revitalization is a unique experience and battle ground. It can feel like you're all alone. But the trials you face are not new. Faithful preachers throughout scriptures and church history have encountered hostility, apathy, and adversity, and continue to do so today. Brian Croft and James Carroll here share their personal stories and seek to encourage you to faithfully persevere in this Spirit-empowered, God-honoring, Christ-exalting work.

Despair, fatigue, and frustration are grave threats to pastoral ministry. How does one not only endure but improve as a preacher when there is little affirmation and few signs of growth? Here is a book that gives advice and inspiration for preachers who need encouragement to stay true to their calling to preach the Word (2 Tim. 4:1).

Joe Barnard
Executive Director, Cross Training Ministries

ISBN 978-1-5271-0382-5

Christian Focus Publications

Our mission statement —

STAYING FAITHFUL

In dependence upon God we seek to impact the world through literature faithful to His infallible Word, the Bible. Our aim is to ensure that the Lord Jesus Christ is presented as the only hope to obtain forgiveness of sin, live a useful life and look forward to heaven with Him.

Our books are published in four imprints:

CHRISTIAN FOCUS

Popular works including biographies, commentaries, basic doctrine and Christian living.

CHRISTIAN HERITAGE

Books representing some of the best material from the rich heritage of the church.

MENTOR

Books written at a level suitable for Bible College and seminary students, pastors, and other serious readers. The imprint includes commentaries, doctrinal studies, examination of current issues and church history.

CF4•K

Children's books for quality Bible teaching and for all age groups: Sunday school curriculum, puzzle and activity books; personal and family devotional titles, biographies and inspirational stories — because you are never too young to know Jesus!

Christian Focus Publications Ltd,
Geanies House, Fearn, Ross-shire,
IV20 1TW, Scotland, United Kingdom.
www.christianfocus.com